Whites Shackled Themselves to Race
and Blacks Have Yet to Free Ourselves

Additional books by Leonce Gaiter

Novels

Bourbon Street

I Dreamt I Was in Heaven

　　– The Rampage of the Rufus Buck Gang

In the Company of Educated Men

Whites Shackled Themselves to Race and Blacks Have Yet to Free Ourselves

LEONCE GAITER

LEGBA BOOKS

Whites Shackled Themselves to Race
and Blacks Have Yet to Free Ourselves

Published by Legba Books
Copyright © 2017 Leonce Gaiter

First edition
ISBN-13: 9780983709312
ISBN-10: 0983709319

For Leonce and Lulene

Table of Contents

Definitions · ix

Preface · xi

Foreword · xv

Introduction—To Culturally Unify DuBois's "Double
Consciousness" · xix

Breaking the 'White' Racial Shackles on the 'Black
Race' · 1

Define "Culture" · 11

Our History Maligned—The Co-Option of the Civil
Rights Movement · 31

Develop the Tools to Resist the White Racial Frame,
or Molder Within It · 51

I Will Happily Disembowel Whoever Next Says "But
We Elected a Black President" · · · · · · · · · · · · · · 58

Programmed for Prejudice: The Biased Norm and
Why We Must Prepare for It · · · · · · · · · · · · · · · 72

Fear of White, or "There Is No Spoon" · · · · · · · · · · · 91

Internalization · 107

In America, Jesus Was a White Man · · · · · · · · · · · · 112

Equal Is Not Good Enough · · · · · · · · · · · · · · · · · · · 133
Historical and Cultural Education on the Jewish
    Model · 138
The Difference between "Black History" and
    "American History from an Afro-American
    Perspective" · 152
A Private Conversation · 165

References · 171

Definitions

African-American—Any American citizen of African ancestry. He or she could be descended from slaves who were brought here in 1700 or be recent Cuban or Ghanaian immigrants who were naturalized yesterday. African-Americans can hail from many different countries and regions and thus may have few, if any, cultural similarities—no more than a recent white German immigrant would have with a recent Italian immigrant. Color is not culture, white or black.

Black—Used interchangeably and synonymous with "African-American."

Afro-American—Denotes the distinct culture of the American descendants of African slaves. This is America's predominant African-American culture and the one that we often mean to invoke when we use the far less specific terms 'black' and "African-American."

Many of the issues that impact Afro-Americans also impact African-Americans more generally. Americans have never been surgical about our prejudice and race hatred. Historically, black skin alone has been enough to trigger it. However, Afro-Americans bear the cultural legacy of America's great crime—slavery and the subsequent 100+ years of both legal and socially accepted apartheid and second-class citizenship, seasoned with terror, violence, and lack of access to educational, political, and financial opportunities that white Americans considered their birthright.

These terms will be used throughout as defined.

Preface

In 2016, a plurality of voting white men and women elevated a man with a long history of racist actions and statements to the highest office in the land, the presidency. American men and women who identify as 'white' elevated a man who had named a white national-ist as his campaign manager. They chose as president a man who wanted to ban an entire religious group from the United States, labeled an entire ethnic group as "rap-ists," prescribed a national program of the "stop and frisk" policies that courts have labeled discriminatory against minorities, and called for the execution of five young black men who had been proven innocent by both DNA evidence and a confession from the real assailant.

With his vulgar, over-the-top, race-baiting demeanor, Donald Trump is a white Louis Farrakhan—a bombastic, autocratic racist. Farrakhan was universally reviled in the press, but Trump was treated respectfully. Why? Because his shtick was so familiar. Yes, he was a fringe figure, but one dragged into the mainstream through particularly deft use of the tools forged by conservatives since the Civil Rights Movement, which a George Wallace campaign aide described as "promise them the moon and holler 'nigger'"—and in this case, epithets for Muslims and Hispanics as well. Trump baked the usual modern conservative cake—bogus claims of voter fraud aimed at minority voters, attacks on "political correctness" as advocacy for full-throated expressions of white supremacy. It was the usual post–civil-rights-era conservative playbook, just with less suit-and-tied respectability. With appeals to race hatred that garnered a loyal following of Klansmen, neo-Nazis, and white supremacists of all stripes, Trump promised everything, from the magical re-emergence of manufacturing jobs to the magical delivery of compromise-free health care, while attacking minorities as undeserving interlopers. "Make America Great Again," was correctly unpacked as code for "Make America White Again."

Watching Trump's rise, I couldn't help thinking that the lessons we took from Martin Luther King and the Civil Rights Movement were wrong.

We refer constantly to America as a land of inclusion, but that's not true and it never has been. In America, "inclusiveness" has always been far more aspirational than actual. For a brief time, after the rights movements of the sixties and early seventies, elites gave lip service to American inclusiveness, but only lip service. Modern conservatism's winks and nods to America's proud history of discrimination and white supremacy has been helping it win statehouses and state legislatures for 50 years—with black faces sprinkled here and there as human shields against their actions being labeled racist. When Barack Obama won the presidency, conservatism's foundational commitment to white supremacy came to the fore. Republicans broke all political norms to thwart Obama's presidency, from tolerating the "birther" lies, to habitual use of the filibuster to block legislation, to shouting "You lie" at a State of the Union Address, to refusing to consider his Supreme Court nominee.

Recent history, culminating in Donald Trump, should finally force black Americans to reject mainstream post–civil-rights-era revisionism glorifying the perfectibility of white people and propping up the lie that black Americans had only to wait for white folks to "come around," that "brotherhood," unicorn-like, would emerge from the mist in the dell to envelop us all in its warmth.

White supremacy is an inescapable nutrient lurking in American soil. Inclusion does not inevitably grow there. Our black skin will always mark us as the people whites evolved their very identity—their pseudo-ethnic 'white' identity—to enslave. And the people adopting this hate-fed identity did so while proclaiming themselves the divinely anointed keepers of fairness and justice.

Can we now—finally—take the first step and free ourselves from the "race" shackles that white Americans clamped on us all those centuries ago—their definition of the black race being negative stereotypes tied to skin color—and define ourselves as the vital American *cultural* force that we have become? Can we then—finally—use that elevated self-image to teach ourselves to live and thrive in the foundationally racist America we have, as opposed to the inclusive fantasy to which a great man sometimes paid lip service and to which the majority delusionally cling? Only then can we move beyond politics and its inevitable focus on redeeming white people and focus instead on ourselves—our history and the culture it's bred—to provide our young the sense of cultural superiority that is the birthright of every child and on which every viable culture propagates itself.

Foreword

Nigger. Negro. Colored. Black. All these terms are sociological, racial identities imposed on us from without. All are the results of whites' economic desire for a permanent source of free labor and their use of negative racial categorization to justify the barbaric system devised to provide it. That system was American chattel slavery. Its viciousness was so extreme that it still afflicts America hundreds of years later.

Having been branded in the late 17th century as a subspecies by the new form of racial categorization, we've spent the remainder of our history ingeniously sloughing off the physical and legal shackles it bred. However, by necessity, we've done it through the lens of that same racial categorization imposed on us. As they chained us, whites insisted that we were no more than the negative traits their racial categorization defined: we were lazy, violent, ignorant—all traits imposed from without to sanction their brutality toward us. Even as we bravely fought those negatives, we accepted the categorization as a racial caste defined largely by our skin color—and by inevitable association, the negativity whites attached to it.

We had nothing else. We were ripped from homelands, cultures, languages, and customs and dropped in a violent, unfamiliar world that insisted we were no more than beasts. We had no power structures through which to insist otherwise. Legally less than true people, we were, nonetheless here. We were present, and so we became a political issue. To most Americans, and to ourselves, we have remained so—not the vibrant cultural force that we've become, but a political issue born of a baseless racial categorization—a fight against a negative racial categorization that has less to do with us and more to do with the majority's historical, violent rapaciousness, subsequent guilt, and desperate measures to further demonize us to reject or absolve themselves of that guilt.

But as with so much else, we elevated our diminished role as a political issue—as opposed to a fully formed people—and mastered the use of politics to fight for our liberation. Throughout, we stopped on occasion to ponder and correct how we referred to ourselves within the racial categorization imposed on us—and the negative attributes associated with it. We evolved from "Negro" to "colored" to "black" to "African-American," but we never fully upended the categorization itself to acknowledge what we had become. We never ripped off the blindfold of the toxic racialist characterization heaped on us. We sought to redeem it in many ways, but we never rejected it. We changed the way we referred to our skin within the sociopolitical spheres of American life, but we always adhered to that 400-year-old racial, skin-based characterization.[a] We were either the people the majority abused and despised, or we were reacting against being abused and despised. We were the legal noncitizens, or we were fighting against our status as legal noncitizens. We were the violent, ignorant beasts or fighting that ugly fantasy. The racial categorization imposed upon us offers only two options, both of which are enslaved to it—succumb or fight against it, both acknowledging its primacy. Either way, the negative, baseless racial characterization wins.

This book looks at the cost of seeing ourselves and this country through the lens imposed upon us centuries ago and how to grow beyond it. The book considers how it's robbed us of what has become the Afro-American cultural birthright that, in this 21st century, we have more than earned. It has prevented us from painting ourselves as the rich historical/cultural force that we have become and passing that portrait on to subsequent generations. Psychologist Margo Monteith said, "To the extent we can feel better about our group relative to other groups, we can feel good about ourselves."[1] Primary adherence to the racist construct of "race" imposed on us centuries

---

a African-American was an improvement, but still bears minimal cultural meaning since Afro-Americans were largely severed from African cultures and Africa is home to hundreds of distinct cultures. African-American simply puts our skin categorization in the broadest geographic context.

ago—as opposed to stepping up to the "culture" that we have become—has kept Afro-Americans from teaching our history and culture to ourselves in a way that elevates us, that provides the necessary sense of cultural superiority, that enables the foundational sense of self-worth required to navigate the often-racist America we face versus the colorblind utopia of which we "have a dream," a dream that Donald Trump's elevation to the presidency and its accompanying crescendo of racist speech and policy has proven is just that in today's America—a dream.

Introduction—To Culturally Unify DuBois's "Double Consciousness"

"After the Egyptian and Indian, the Greek and Roman, the Teuton and Mongolian, the Negro is a sort of seventh son, born with a veil, and gifted with second-sight in this American world,—a world which yields him no true self-consciousness, but only lets him see himself through the revelation of the other world. It is a peculiar sensation, this double-consciousness, this sense of always looking at one's self through the eyes of others, of measuring one's soul by the tape of a world that looks on in amused contempt and pity. One ever feels his twoness,—an American, a Negro; two souls, two thoughts, two unreconciled strivings; two warring ideals

*in one dark body, whose dogged strength
alone keeps it from being torn asunder."*

—W.E.B. DuBois, *The Souls
of Black Folk*, 1903

Born in 1958, I was raised to think I had something to prove. I was raised to preempt the images my skin would invoke in the whites (and blacks) around me. My father was a military officer, my mother a schoolteacher. During the early 1960s, before the zenith of the Civil Rights Movement, they were stationed all over the country and sometimes abroad. Both Southern and black, they had no illusions about the white men and women with whom they shared workplaces and neighborhoods. They knew they had to protect themselves from anything that would allow the finger-on-the-trigger white minds around them to think the ever-threatened "Nigger." They avoided anything that would make whites think, much less utter, that ever-looming epithet. Once uttered, the effect was inescapable. It was a death sentence without appeal. Thus labeled subhuman, you could not snatch back your humanity; you could not retaliate in kind—there was no such name to similarly dehumanize and humiliate whites. That word would poison the well between my parents and their workplace peers and superiors—the people upon whom they depended for their livelihoods.

My parents lived in fear. They lived DuBois's famous "double consciousness." They were always looking at themselves through the eyes of whites to ensure that they and their children remained impeccable, above reproach, miles from "Nigger." White kids could act up, act out, play with abandon, skirt the rules, let off steam, shout, holler, run around in bare feet and dirty clothes, but I could not. A laughing, dirty white child was playing. A laughing dirty black one was a pickaninny. A white kid in a fight was being a kid. A black kid fighting was a savage. Always, "Nigger" lay in wait, and "Nigger" could affect my parents' ability to gain advancement, make money and provide us with a middle class life, and the opportunity to finally, the idea went, educate ourselves out of having to consider that word.

We lived in fear. Every day. Every time we stepped outside our door. Fear of the accusatory white minds all around us and fear of the learned self-loathing they could inflame with just a single word. It was as if we'd been brainwashed and programmed to question our worth and the validity of our very existence at the utterance of "Nigger." As DuBois put it, "*measuring one's soul by the tape of a world that looks on in amused contempt and pity.*"

I endured the "double consciousness" for half of my life.

With my parents' boundless 1960s ambitions for their children, we attended principally white schools since they were generally the best available. During my time, we lived in principally white neighborhoods because they most often gave access to those good schools. I went to Harvard, then into the film and television industries, and then on to high-tech marketing. White schools, white workplaces, white neighborhoods. My life has been an inadvertent anthropological study of white Americans and their reactions to me as a black man living among them. What I experienced taught me about the depths and breadth of American prejudice and the painful power of the black self-images born from it. It also taught me the possibility of rejecting both and unifying the double consciousness into a single Afro-American *cultural* outlook that denies me nothing of America—for all of it is mine—and nothing of Afro-America (save the negative images whites passed down in tandem with their racial categorizations).

From late elementary school to college, most of my friends were Jewish. I watched them, in their tweens and teens, prepare for Bar Mitzvahs and Bat Mitzvahs, saw the cultural immersion they received from other Jews. They were culturally different and acknowledged themselves as such. They held that difference dear. Hot on the heels of early childhood, they were taught to cherish their difference. From other Jews, they learned their history, the Holocaust, diaspora, the birth of Israel—all from other Jews. This was their religion, their culture, and they asked no one else to validate it. They asked no one else's permission to teach it in whatever way they saw fit, and they cared no more than necessary what others did or did not know about it—all this despite age-old persecution.

I wondered why there was no such systematic, organized historical and cultural education for American descendants of African slaves, though our unique historical place, distinct cultural heritage, and history of oppression seemed to demand it. Only later would I lay the blame at the feet of continued reliance on the political, racialist categorization on which Afro-Americans still inordinately rely and liberation movements that never grew past it.

With a cultural education at the feet of other African-Americans, akin to the Jewish model, black children would learn the truth about the reception they can expect as they march through their lives in this country. They would be inoculated against much of the prejudice they encounter; they would be less likely to internalize it. They would be armed to know the hows and whys of our place in this nation. They would learn what every other functional culture teaches its young—who they are, the gifts with which they have been blessed, the burdens they will suffer, and why they stand second to no one.

Right now, we relegate this function to schools teaching curricula largely created by and for those who have spent an American history oppressing and belittling us.

Why?

A study by Ming-Te Wang and James P. Huguley of the University of Pittsburgh and Harvard, respectively, found that children of parents who practice "cultural socialization"—the process of instilling racial pride, history, and tradition, as well as "preparation for bias," which prepares children to encounter racial prejudice—show better outcomes in grade point average (GPA), educational aspirations, and the ability to think critically using analysis and problem solving.

> *"Our examination of the moderating effects of racial socialization practices suggests that parents' messages to their children regarding positive aspects of group membership (pride, history, and tradition) attenuate the negative effects of teacher discrimination on both GPA and educational aspirations.*
>
> *"These findings suggest that cultural socialization and preparation for bias practices interact to make uniquely positive contributions to the education aspirations and school identification of African American adolescents. "*[2]

To provide an expansive vision of Afro-America that allows us to better thrive in this country, we must color outside the lines of the racial classification to which we've adhered throughout our history—even within triumphant moments like the Civil Rights Movement. It demands that we move past merely rejecting racist views born of that classification and shatter the classification itself, thereby sanctioning our possession of everything this country has to offer instead of complying with the notion that most of it is "theirs"—that they hold a more central place in its history and formation than we—that they bear more credit for its status than we—that they can have a right to more of its fruits than we.

I want to reclaim Afro-American history and its attendant culture for Afro-Americans, outside the confines of the bargain basement bin in which American history relegates "black history." I want choices clearly available outside of mimicking or accepting mainstream racist myths or a lifetime of reacting to them. I want to destroy in the black mind the notion of 'whiteness' outside an overtly racist context and thus open the entirety of this nation, its history and culture, to Afro-American exploitation— because all of it is ours. By shedding reliance on the racist racial categories that have bound us with ropes made of the majority's self-imposed whiteness—and the bigotry the identity was created to foster—we can finally blind the contemptuous "eyes of others" of which the double consciousness speaks.

Breaking the 'White' Racial
Shackles on the 'Black Race'

*"When the first Africans arrived in Virginia
in 1619, there were no white people there."*

—Theodore Allen

*"The result of genetic research on 'race' is that
there is no biological basis for human race."*

—American Museum of Natural History

*"The white race is a historically
constructed social formation. It consists
of all those who partake of the privileges
of the white skin in this society."*

—Noel Ignatiev

*"Adopting and treasuring a white identity
is absolutely a moral choice, since there are*

no white people. . . . As long as you think
you're white, there is no hope for you."

—JAMES BALDWIN

There is no genetic basis for race. Race is a social construct, not a biological one. Science has proven that there is more variation within so-called racial groups than between them. The Human Genome Project proved that humans share 99.99% of their genes, regardless of their so-called "race." "And of that tiny 0.1% difference, 94 per cent of the variation is among individuals from the same populations and only six percent between individuals from different populations."[3] That means that only 6% of 0.1% represents variances between different populations or so-called races.

Thus, the idea of identifying consistent genetic differentiations between groups that represent quantifiable behavioral distinctions that we choose to call 'black' or 'white' is pseudoscientific nonsense. We have never even concretely identified what a 'black' person is. What level of specific genetic material qualifies one as 'black?' We can't answer that, so we rely on self-identification, which is unscientific in the extreme. I have had relatives who make Meryl Streep look dusky but who define themselves as 'black.' Throughout the centuries, light skinned Afro-Americans with two visibly 'black' parents have passed as 'white.' Again, the concept of race as we colloquially understand it is ridiculous.

Why, then, do we constantly refer to ourselves as 'black' or 'white'?

For most of this nation's history, race has defined America. However, there was a time prior to this country's founding when the 'white race' did not exist. For his book *The Invention of the White Race*, Theodore Allen scoured records from 17th-century Virginia, where almost one in four bond laborers was of African origin. He found no use of the word 'white' in official records until around 1680. Thus, from 1619 to around 1680, despite the presence of both black and white indentured laborers in Virginia, no one was officially categorized or described as 'white.'

> *"Winthrop D. Jordan, author of White Over Black, found that, 'After about 1680, taking the colonies as a whole, a new term appeared—"white." During my own study of page after page of Virginia county records, reel after reel of microfilm prepared by the Virginia Colonial Records Project, and other seventeenth-century sources, I have found no instance of the official use of the word "white" as a token of social status before its appearance in a Virginia law passed in 1691, referring to 'English or other white women'"*[4]

Allen points out that until the latter 17th century, the term 'white' was not universally accepted and had to be defined for English audiences.

"English ship captain Richard Jobson made a trading voyage to Africa in 1620-21, but he refused to engage in trafficking in human beings, because, he said, the English 'were a people who did not deal in any such commodities, neither did we buy or sell one another or any that had our own shapes.' When the local dealer insisted that it was the custom there to sell Africans 'to white men,' Jobson answered 'they [that is 'white men'] were another kinde of people from us.' George Fox, founder of the Quaker religion, in 1671 addressed some members of a Barbados congregation as 'you that are called white.' Another seventeenth-century commentator, Morgan Godwyn, found it necessary to explain to the English at home that, in Barbados, 'white' was 'the general name for Europeans.'"[5]

Thus, during a time when black bonded servants were often treated similarly to white ones, with evidence of cooperation between the groups, the term 'white' was neither prominent nor used to describe an official category of person. At that time, on what would become American soil, the 'white race' had yet to be established.

That does not mean that the inevitable human failing of prejudice against the odd-looking "other" that presaged and paved the way for chattel slavery did not exist. Allen termed the state of Africans vs. Europeans in 17th-century Chesapeake as "indeterminate":

"A 1661 law specifying punishment for runaway bond-laborers referred to 'any negroes who are incapable of

makeing satisfaction by addition of time.' In 1668, free African-American women were declared tithable (taxable as laborers, a condition from which European women were exempt) on the explicit grounds that 'though permitted to enjoy their freedome . . . [they] ought not in all respects be admitted to a full fruition of the exemptions and immunities of the English.'"[6]

Only with the economic desire to degrade Africans to the role of property did the 'white race' become established. Slave owners had to define a permanent class of persons as so different from themselves that they did not deserve the right to own their own bodies, the fruits of their labors, or their own offspring. This group of humans would hold the status of horses or dogs. They had to be defined as so distinct from slave owners of pale skin, so beneath them, that they deserved no better than their perpetual enslavement. The dark skinned had to be the opposite of the slave owners. And so the 'white race' was born to distinguish itself by solely imbuing 'whites' with the attributes of humanity and blacks with those of beasts.

Our enslavement so impacted this nation, was so central to its existence, that all its majority soon adopted a 'white' racial identity to cement their full humanity. Only that identity ensured their access to freedom. For poor whites, that identity also provided something new and precious—a political, social, and cultural tether to the landed wealthy—a connection that did not exist in class-based European societies, a connection that helped grow the American ideal of upward mobility. In Europe, gentlefolk were akin to a different species from the poor. The poor were a lesser breed by birth. They weren't *sub*-humans, just *lesser* ones. They were born to and expected to die in "their place."

Suddenly, as 'white,' the poor shared a bond with the wealthy—they were both 'white' and thus superior to the true subhuman—dark-skinned men and women. There was suddenly a bridge from one group—the poor—to another—the wealthy, between whom there'd previously been an unbridgeable chasm. Suddenly, one could fathom traveling from one to the other, for they now had a common bond and cause—'whiteness.'

W.E.B. DuBois wrote of poor whites overseeing black slaves:

> "It gave him work and some authority as overseer, slave driver, and member of the patrol system. But above and beyond this, it fed his vanity because it associated him with the masters. Slavery bred in the poor white a dislike of Negro toil of all sorts. He never regarded himself as a laborer, or as part of any labor movement. If he had any ambition at all it was to become a planter and to own 'niggers.'"[7]

Consider that the need to denigrate the African slave as subhuman helped give rise to the American ideal of upward mobility—one that we hold precious to this day.

It is fitting irony that in the early 21st century, the loss of that ideal of upward mobility—the untethering of the working class from the gentry that we now call the 1%—has led the white working class down a racist, nativist path, as evidenced by the late 20th-century Republican party and the Trumpism it birthed. The great untethering has led those who embrace a traditional white identity on a frightening quest to reclaim the hate-based glory of that designation.

Everything a human could want, any opportunity for "life, liberty and the pursuit of happiness," became contingent on being white. To be other than white was to be degraded, to be less than human.

Pseudoscience soon worked to provide this new racial categorization the patina of respectability. Scholars using Adam and Eve as points of human origin and genetically segregating the aristocracy from the rabble presaged the racist 20th-century theories of "The Bell Curve," and the 21st-century theories of "A Troublesome Inheritance."

Today, we can barely discuss any aspect of this country or its history without relying on distinctions born of the toxic brew of savage greed and vicious human prejudice that drove the majority to erroneously declare themselves a separate race—the 'white race.' Politics, health care, arts, religion—all are thoroughly infused with race-based distinctions born of the majority's need to subhumanize their dark-skinned slave population.

Something Happened—Something Cultural

Those who declared themselves 'white' made it easy to view the Africans they imported as subhuman. Torn from homeland, language, religion, relations, we were dropped in a new world like traumatized newborns. Further brutalities endemic to American slavery further stunted us. We were not allowed to speak native languages, learn to read or write, worship, marry, or rear our young to anything other than slavery.

But something happened. Even with our lowly status born from the aberrant power of white racial identity, we began to distinguish ourselves *culturally*. We took the religion we were handed (with its white Gods) and reshaped some of it to speak to our lust for freedom. We married the music recalled from homelands with the music absorbed here to create something new. Fresh modes of speech and expression grew from our boundless ingenuity.

We took the empty, violent self-adulation of the fictional 'white race' and redeemed its opposite—us— into a distinct American subculture that has grown to dominate not only America itself but, in multiple arenas, the world. Today in America, when we refer to "black religion" or "black music" or black anything else, we are rarely referring to music made by recent émigré Liberians or Somalis. We are talking about music born of the American descendants of American slaves. Black religion is the religion born of the American descendants of

African slaves. Black idioms are modes of speech born of the American descendants of African slaves. We maintained the ugly, race-based terminology necessitated by the majority's self-expulsion from the human race to become the 'white race' but pulled from it modes of speech, worship, music, movement, and letters that have enlightened the world. We developed the most distinctive and distinguished of American subcultures, but defined it via the only lens historically available to us, the one DuBois described as providing "no true self-consciousness," letting us see ourselves only through "the revelation of the other world" that looks down on us in "amused contempt and pity."

That lens, that racial frame in which we were introduced to this land and through which we've been seen throughout its history, insisted that we see ourselves through a 'white racial' point of view even if our goal was to see past that point of view. Looking through the lens of the 'white race,' we could view ourselves only in opposition to their view of us—which inherently places a primary value on the point of view you must constantly work to shun. For most of this nation's history, we certainly could not principally define ourselves as a unique American cultural force born of African roots, slavery, liberation, segregation, and political and social rebellion. Thus, the race-based, cultureless "Nigger," "Colored," "Negro," and "Black" predominated. We made progress with "African-American" since it made a broad swipe at tying us to a place and its cultural tradition—it was just the wrong tradition, so tied were we to categories that denied us a place within the American tapestry.

Now, it's possible—no, imperative—to move beyond the lens of the fictitious 'white race,' beyond the holographic wall it imposed between us and this country's mainstream wealth. It is time because that mainstream is ours; it owes as much to us as it does to them. Without our seeing the world through their 'white' racial lens, their seeming ownership of this land evaporates. Without seeing ourselves in their White Racial Frame, the negativity of the double consciousness evaporates. We are no longer watching them look at us and seeing ourselves through their eyes, and reacting in some form or another to what they see. Through taking ownership of our rightful cultural place as a primary source of the best of America, we gain the ability to see this land through our own eyes, to see the distinctly American cultural treasure that is Afro-America, and place every one of us at its heart.

Define "Culture"

Webster's Ninth Edition—5a. the integrated pattern of human knowledge, belief, and behavior that depends upon man's capacity for learning and transmitting knowledge to succeeding generations. 5b. the customary beliefs, social forms, and material traits of a racial, religious, or social group.

Skin colors don't create cultures. Only peoples with histories do that. By kidnapping us from indigenous cultures and subsequently categorizing us as less than human, as nothing more than physical features tied to negative attributes, whites denied us a place at the American table, with the intent of denying us a place in American history. They also intended to deny us the right to create a history of our own. We were property. We had nothing of our own. America was theirs. We were no more than skin-wrapped tools that wept and bled.

Come Jim Crow, freed from slavery, the denial of our rights continued. Denial of the vote, political representation, and equal justice was designed to prolong our omission from benefiting from or contributing to American history.

The majority besmirched this country's ideals and used every mechanism at their disposal to deny us the right to create a history.

We did it anyway.

* * *

Let's look at American history and culture, which blacks, whites, Jews, Hispanics, Catholics, Asians, Muslims, and all other Americans share. We have our enduring creation myths: the American Revolutionary War was about freedom from tyranny, our Founding Fathers' belief that all men are "created equal," George Washington as a uniquely brilliant military strategist, to name a few. Regardless of the degree to which we accept these myths, as Americans, we imbibe them, and at some point in our lives, accept them. They bind us (to the extremely limited degree we are bound) as Americans. The history surrounding them is part of our public education. We pass this knowledge from generation to generation.

This knowledge—this culture—belongs as much to me, a black man, as it does to any white man or woman. However, much of it lives in opposition to, and therefore in contempt of, my Afro-American history and thus my ability to mold a fully positive conception of self.

Founders fighting tyranny qualifies as irony—they owned *slaves*—as does unquestioningly accepting the nobility of the statement "All men are created equal" when some men were property whose owners could maim or kill them on a whim as legally as they could shatter a similarly owned vase.

For Afro-Americans to fully accept these American historical and cultural myths is to accept our immutable insignificance. To accept them is to insist that there is no irony in slavers crying for freedom or espousing equality for all but you. One can only cry freedom in the midst of slavery by ignoring the enslaved.

Afro-American writer Albert Murray referred to the American descendants of African slaves as "Omni-Americans." He said that our "heroic philosophy of improvisation and adaptation epitomized the national character at its most refined" and that American culture was "'incontestably mulatto': American song, speech, humor, dance and folklore were all thoroughly infused with black idioms."[8] To Murray, we are the through line of American history.

He was right, and it's time to acknowledge in the popular Afro-American mind that we have now lived a vital history in this country, much of which exists in opposition to the mainstream culture to which we are all exposed. To be blunt, in the physics of American myths, we are the anti(mythical)americans. Our history bears the opposite charge to the majority's myth matter. We negate significant portions of it. Creative destruction of mainstream

American myths is a vital part of our history, which distinguishes it from mainstream history. That distinction is crucial to us as a people, for without it, we are prone to be partially erased in our own minds. Trump supporters voted to "Make America Great Again," emphasis on "again," signifying an acceptance of the myth that America was great when its majority waded nose deep in the offal of their race hatred born of their self-expulsion from the human race to join the 'white race.'

This history we've made over the centuries differs from that of the majority. That's why the culture that stems from it differs as well; that is why we must devise systems to take ownership of it and teach it to ourselves.

* * *

To thrive in America, Afro-Americans must be *of* mainstream American culture. We must know it inside and out. We must know the history and customs and mores that grew from it—if only to deflect the arrows they fling at us to preserve an often-racist status quo. We should know it because Albert Murray was right: Laura Nyro and Charles Ives are mine as much as they are any other American's. I know the American history that they lived and the American culture in which they lived as well as any white man or woman.

But then, I also have jazz great Charles Mingus. If whites want him, he can be theirs as well. He is part of their culture too. But with that great man, I share a history and Afro-American culture that will forever be out of reach for most non–Afro-Americans. Just as I, for instance, will never know what it means to be a Native American and watch a typical Hollywood Western or hear a traditional language, few whites will ever fully understand the culture that I share with Mingus and I hear in his music. Yes, I can appreciate the lie of the traditional Hollywood Western as well as a Native American. I can empathize to a point with the pain that it could inflict to see one's indigenous culture portrayed as the interloper, the usurper, but I will never have the experience watching that film that a man or woman of that culture will have because I am not *of* their culture.

Similarly, there are experiences of things Afro-American and black that will forever be out of reach for most others. I have a friend who is obsessed with classic R&B. Knows it backward and sideways. Yet he never fully understood (as in *felt* viscerally) that Aretha Franklin's place was not just musical, but cultural. Hollering "Freedom" in 1967 through every radio in America meant more to blacks than it did to him. To us, it was intuitively political, cultural, and personal. To him, it was spectacular music. As Afro-Americans, we share a slice of America that is out of reach to most. Yet mainstream America and its culture are ours as much as anyone's because we can eat and drink it from birth alongside every American man and woman. The only aspect of mainstream culture that should be out of our reach is its disdain for us and ours—that is, America's historical race hatred. (Unfortunately, we imbibe a good amount of that as well.) Such access to two cultures demands that we embrace the additional burden of teaching ourselves our own history, comings, goings, and the ways of being they have bred in us, even as we also learn all that the majority learn.

This might be asking the extraordinary of Afro-Americans. But this book is about accomplishing the extraordinary. It is about finally dispelling fears, self-doubts, and insecurities born of a racist, color-based history of this . . .

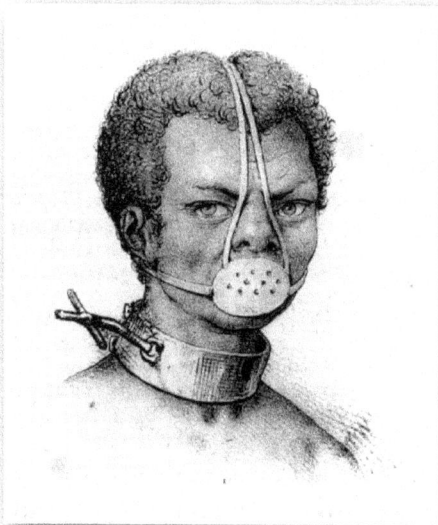

Figure 1 – Slave in iron muzzle

and this . . .

Figure 2 – Omaha race riot lynching of Will Brown, 1919

Figure 3 – Segregated swimming pool sign from Selma, Alabama

and this . . .

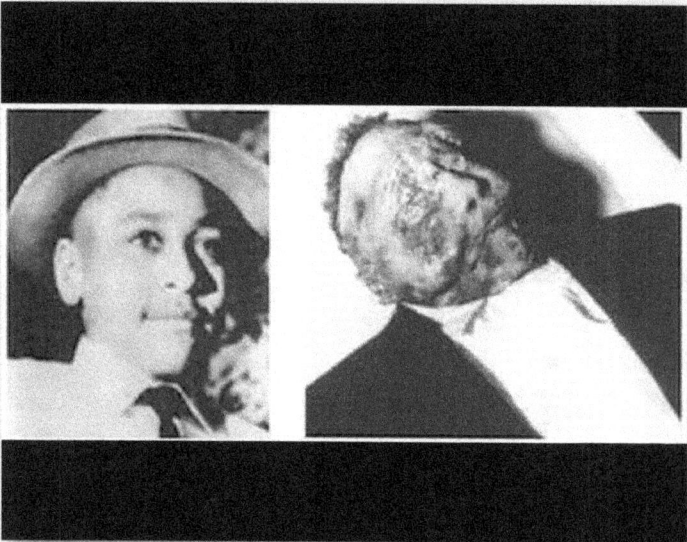

Figure 4 – Emmett Till before and after
his brutal lynching in 1955

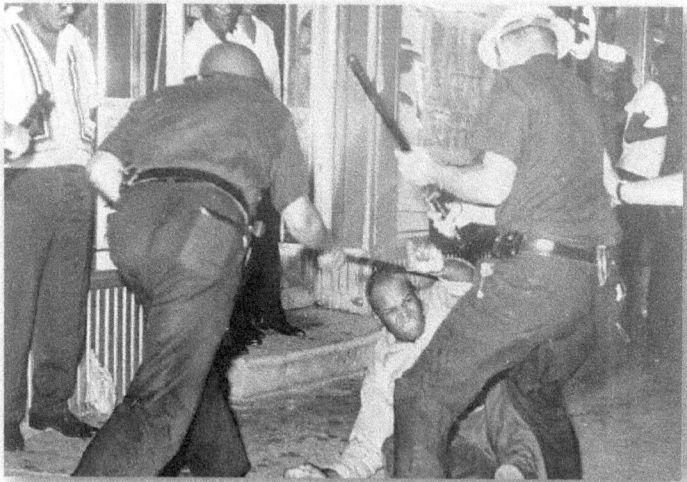

Figure 5 – Civil rights protester being beaten

Figure 6 – Florida Klan rally, 1970s

and this . . .

Figure 7 – Eric Garner killed by NYPD officers
for selling loose cigarettes in 2014

Rational fears born of experience have led so many Afro-Americans to reject major swaths of the "main-stream" to the point that we don't vote in sufficient numbers, which leads directly to racist policies like stop and frisk, voter suppression, and an unjust justice system. Yes, such rejection of the mainstream is understandable. How do you acknowledge that there is something poisonous in the very culture that literally helped create you while simultaneously embracing that same culture? How do you acknowledge that your existence as a cultural being is due in part to your countrymen's contempt for you? How do you reconcile your fear, and yes, sometimes, hatred of the majority culture for sins it committed and tolerated for so long, with an embrace and mastery of that culture?

These are not esoteric questions. They have enormous real-world consequences. In 2016, Hillary Clinton lost Michigan by about 10,000 votes. Voter turnout in Detroit and Wayne County was 75,000 voters shy of the 2012 turnout.[9] Matching the 2012 turnout in those regions could have won the state for Clinton. That pattern was similar in Wisconsin and elsewhere. Many blacks stayed home (one hopes) not realizing that by doing so, they voted for cops being able to shoot their unarmed black sons, grandsons, and daughters without facing justice. Not realizing that they were condemning their children to suffer the racist humiliations of stop and frisk and endure emboldened racists openly calling them "monkey" and "nigger" in schools and colleges. Not realizing they would endure even greater voter suppression and suffer minimized protections against racial discrimination, thus potentially sentencing themselves and their children to substandard jobs, loans, schools, and opportunities. Staying home in 2016, for whatever reason, was a tacit endorsement—a passive vote for—a white supremacist America. The rural whites who turned out in droves knew this and voted for the benefit of their adopted, historically racist white identities. Too many of us, lulled to somnolence by the fantasy of "inclusive" America, the dream that the justice and fairness will out, stayed home. The fact that they didn't know enough of our American history to realize the stakes is no one's fault but our own. How could they know? We never taught them. And no one else will.

Arrogant, Uppity, and Then Some

"Transmitting knowledge to succeeding generations." What knowledge about our distinct subculture do Afro-Americans customarily transmit in an organized fashion from generation to generation? I remember consistently seeing the book *To Be a Jew* on the bookshelves of my high school friends. They had to study and learn about their culture to be formally welcomed into it and into adulthood. For boys, it was the Bar Mitzvah, for girls, the Bat Mitzvah. For many Jews, the symbology is as much cultural as it is religious.

There was no such book in my house regarding being an American descendant of African slaves. I wish there had been. I wish I had had access to a source of American history and culture from an Afro-American perspective. However, I did have some sources of cultural strength. First, I was raised during my parents' rise to the comfortable middle class through my father's promotion in the military, one of the least segregated economic sectors at the time, and my mother's second income as an elementary school teacher. Second, I was 10 in 1968 and living in Washington, DC, which was full of middle class blacks. The Civil Rights Movement had reached its zenith and begun its dissolution into more amorphous rights movements and antiwar protests, and Afro-American life, history, culture, practice, and theory were alive in the air all around me. Finally, my mother was born of a distinct subculture within the Afro-American culture that afforded her many of the benefits I hope for Afro-America at large: a sense of self-worth, entitlement, and yes, even cultural superiority.

My mother was raised a black New Orleans Creole. That means she was part of an upper caste in Afro-American society dating back hundreds of years. These were half-breeds and quadroons considered tainted by their black blood, but afforded special status and privilege due to their light skin. They were the descendants of white slave masters and overseers, and they seized their special status to become more prosperous than darker-skinned blacks, to use the race hatred all around them to their advantage—though still crimped and frustrated by the hatred they too faced.

Their ability to attain their status was based on a grotesque, colorist belief: the closer to white, the better you were. However, Creoles wrested from this baseness a society they considered as cultured as the white, while taking their place as the elite of the black. In addition, they seem to have considered themselves prettier than either and were not above holding both in contempt.

It was my good fortune (and sometimes misfortune) to be born into such arrogance, to be the progeny of people who somehow managed to consider themselves more clever, more resourceful, and more wise than those around them due to their unique history and place in society—despite all the lies, half-truths, and racist contradictions their place bespoke. Thus, I had a leg up in the battle to slough off the contempt of the majority—the equation of beauty with white skin, of intelligence with white minds, of normality with straight hair. A leg up, I say; I was not immune. No black man, woman, or child is immune to such a dehumanizing deluge. You react. The question is, will that reaction ultimately hinder you or propel you forward? And what tools do you need to achieve the latter?

The tools required are those that deconstruct our conception of ourselves as a racial caste and political issue instead of a cultural entity. We need to acknowledge that we have become one of this nation's most fruitful cultural mines while failing to use that culture to do much other than entertain and amuse our ourselves and our countrymen. We have not used it to do what other sustaining cultures do—teach ourselves our own history and traditions and our cultural contributions and value, and how to wield them to navigate successfully in the larger, often-racist society. When we do that, we will no longer be buffeted between the rock and the hard place of DuBois's hundred-year-old double conscioussness, but enveloped in a history told from our own point of view and a grand appreciation of the critical American culture we've pulled from it.

There are multiple reasons we have never done that, but the first surrounds the ethos that has grown from the ashes of the Civil Rights Movement.

Black Americans: Still Believers in the Perfectibility of Whites

Published in the Los Angeles Times, *February 5, 1995*
(Copyright The Times Mirror Company; Los Angeles Times 1995. All Rights reserved)

Conservatives, moderates and liberals alike (black and white) now hurl "pull yourself up by your bootstraps" bromides at the black community. Bill Clinton stands before black Baptist congregations extolling the virtues of "personal responsibility." These cons, mods and libs often claim (sometimes rightly) that old-style, '60s, liberal Great Society programs have not yielded adequate results, and that some of the programs have proved counterproductive. Some, particularly the black ones, insist that a "culture of dependence" has caused African Americans to hitch their stars to the government's supposedly benevolent wagon.

What these politicians and pundits fail to see is that they're viewing the situation through the most narrow of lenses. The whole truth is more frightening, because the acknowledgment of it demands enormous changes in the way black Americans view our minority selves in this majority culture. The whole truth is that black Americans are the ultimate American Dreamers. Despite a history that should have taught us better, we still believe in the Constitution. We still believe in the perfectibility of this Republic, of its political and popular culture with respect to us, both of which are most identifiably embodied in the form of the (ever demonized) "White Man."

Our problem is that we still believe. We believe more in the perfectibility of "them" than we do in the perfectibility of ourselves. We are the last American Dreamers, the last of the true believers.

Perhaps we learned our Christian lessons too well. The civil-rights movement boasted more than its share of reverends. To this day, "reverend" is the most common title for black men (they always are) accorded the mantle of "black leader." Historically, the reverends were the most educated and worldly men in the pre-civil-rights-era black community. They performed a myriad of tasks. When it came time to demand our rights within the broader culture, we looked to the reverends for leadership. And we got it.

The Rev. Martin Luther King Jr. became the most visible symbol of the movement. His tactical skills were regularly overshadowed by his verbal gifts, which were formed and infused by his sense of Christian mission. King preached to us, to all of America, of her own perfectibility. He made the sins of the majority popular culture—its bigotry, its violence against black citizens—seem so much biblical waywardness, which he, in true Christian fashion, was willing to forgive and forget. He offered America and her people Christian absolution for their sins—literal and political.

America prepared to do penance—political, not personal—penance for those sins. The Great Society was that penance. America would make amends.

I often hear expressions of sadness and wonderment that the civil-rights movement failed to achieve the lasting sea-change in race relations that it seemed to portend. Stereotypes still rage, wages still lag, banks continue to redline, white flight still occurs, the suggestion (always erroneous) that most recipients of any government benefit are predominantly black is sufficient to guarantee support for the abolition of that benefit (when much grander give-aways to all white recipients go unnoticed). In some ways, it seems that little has changed.

In many ways, little has. The civil-rights movement asked precious little. A deeply Christian man and the crusade he symbolized were warmly embraced by a large portion of white America for all the wrong reasons: namely, that the movement preached the perfectibility of the majority and of the society over which they hold sway.

Regarded thus, King becomes a grandly tragic figure with a touch of Ellingtonian plaintiveness about him. His deeply moral beliefs were taken to the hearts of many for self-aggrandizing reasons—less that they could truly claim a lack of prejudice or truly sought to attain such a state, and more a desire to celebrate their own perfectibility without the attendant work of changing the foundation of the way they think. Any non-black individual was welcome to believe that no black person was his or her equal (to believe someone your equal means you acknowledge their potential superiority to you in any given endeavor), but they could join the crowd in saying that the inferior should be treated kindly.

The government offered to make amends, and we (black Americans) believed in the constitutional connection between a government and its people, a connection that has been eroding for at least 30 years, and one in which not even the staunchest flag-waver could believe after the bloodletting of the 1994 political season. We believed that the government actions represented the will of its people. We believed in the goodwill of our countrymen based upon the displays of their "representative" government.

We believed so much that we made the naturally illogi-cal progression to looking to the government to sway its people, looking to political change to stimulate cultural change, asking the cart to pull the horse under the best circumstances—in the forms of, for instance, busing and affirmative action.

The outrageous extent to which we believed was both painfully and poignantly apparent in a journalistic cause celebre a couple of years back. A Yale-educated black law-yer made a big splash with a New York Magazine article in which he chronicled his weeklong exploit as a busboy in a posh lily-white country club. The headline asked why this $105,000-a-year Yale lawyer took a $7-an-hour job as a busboy at the snootiest, whitest country club in Connecticut.

The writer became a mini cause celebre by allowing white readers to feign righteous shock that rich white people uttered the word "nigger" inside an all-white country club. Both the principally white readership and the black writer's noble reaction to this shocking news—their crudely choreographed dance of indignation—rested upon their mutual assumption of the inherent goodness of white Americans, their inherent fairness toward their black brethren. Only from this assumption could one be shocked that members of a racist club behaved like racists inside it.

This highly educated, intelligent, successful man believed so much in the perfectibility of "them" that he expressed shock that these people weren't "good" people. He believed so much—in them.

We still believe. Unfortunately, we have made meals of the majority's contempt for so long, we keep believing in "them," in "it," be it a government, an African past from which we were severed hundreds of years ago as completely as a people could be—anything but our black American selves.

The Afro-American desire (no, demand) for equal access to the fruits of American society is one thing. Putting common sense aside and asking why white people don't just love us is another. It is the securing of effective access routes to America's fruits, based on realities at hand, on which Afro-Americans should concentrate our efforts. Belief is laudable, particularly in martyrs, but it has limited practical applications. We have focused all our extravagant attentions on "The White Man"—getting him or her to change or behave properly—too little on effectively using our own cultural strengths and capital to navigate this particular American racial minefield.

Damn the concept of The White Man—a concept as racist as The Black Man (one can't utter the former reduction without succumbing to the reductions inherent in the latter). There are quiet revolutions going on all about us. The middle class shrinks, the industrial laborer disappears, the work force becomes mobile, the two-party system weakens, the American Dream fades. It is a time for upheaval. Let's start with US this time; and then teach the rest of us (the majority) to see us as we really are, not as its cultural prejudice distorts us—rather than believing so hard that we beg, prod and plead for "them" to change when they have no impetus to do so, save their inherent goodness; and crying and screaming when they do not.

Our History Maligned—The Co-Option of the Civil Rights Movement

Quote #1:

"I refuse to accept the view that mankind is so tragically bound to the starless midnight of racism and war that the bright daybreak of peace and brotherhood can never become a reality. . . . I believe that unarmed truth and unconditional love will have the final word."

Quote #2:

"The thing wrong with America is white racism. White folks are not right. . . . It's time for America to have an intensified study on what's wrong with white folks."

Quote #3:

"It is an unhappy truth that racism is a way of life for the vast majority of white Americans, spoken and

unspoken, acknowledged and denied, subtle and some-
times not so subtle—the disease of racism permeates and
poisons a whole body politic. And I can see nothing more
urgent than for America to work passionately and unre-
lentingly—to get rid of the disease of racism.

"Something positive must be done. Everyone must
share in the guilt as individuals and as institutions. The
government must certainly share the guilt; individuals
must share the guilt; even the church must share the guilt."

All quotes above are from Martin Luther King. The MLK of the first quote represents the benevolent Christian preacher who, per mainstream thinking, worked not to secure the civil rights of black Americans, but to redeem all Americans through love and brotherhood. He is the man who preached the forever-impending perfectibility of whites, awaiting the day when they would no longer see the color of our skin—the day they would be struck colorblind.

The MLK of the second and third quotes was the Afro-American familiar with the comorbid diseases of white supremacy and race hatred that afflict American society, a man who was willing to kill (as in take actions that would lead to loss of life) or die to fight against tenets the majority held dear, to kill or die to fight against the policies and practices of the mighty U.S. government and against the conservative element in the black community itself.

Both men were Martin Luther King. But politicians and opinion makers lionize only one—the first. The majority choose to remember only one—the first. The majority choose to teach their children (and ours) about only one—the first—if they teach them much of anything at all.

The elite, popular conception of Martin Luther King and the Civil Rights Movement ranges from the white centric to the perverse. In an article titled "Why I'm Tired of Hearing About 'That' Civil Rights Movement," John Blake of CNN identifies what he calls three damaging myths about the Civil Rights Movement. The first is, "It was a black thang."

> *"A quick word association test," Blake wrote. "When you hear the words civil rights, what kind of faces do you see? Only black? As I talked to various groups about the movement, I gradually realized that it was primarily seen as a black struggle instead of an American movement that helped all sorts of people."*[10]

Blake is right. Whites played significant roles in the Movement. The Civil Rights Movement also seeded additional rights movements. However, for blacks and the majority of whites, it was, in fact, a "black thing." Our rights were denied; we started it, and we overwhelmingly peopled and propelled it. The majority of the white population did not approve of it. Sixty percent did not approve of the March on Washington, thinking it would lead to violence. In 1963, 78% of whites said they would move from a neighborhood if a black family moved in.

Reassigning the Civil Rights Movement from primarily an Afro- and African-American struggle to claim our rights to an "American movement that helped all sorts of people" is a thinly veiled insult to the black men, women, and children of that movement—as great an insult as it would be to deny that whites played roles in it. More importantly, doing so robs us of the basic cultural authority to view our history from our own point of view. It denies us cultural ownership of a cultural touchstone. It denies us the right to be the heroes of our own history. I'm sure it sounds to the majority very "patriotic" and inclusive to talk of the Civil Rights Movement as a national kumbaya moment, but that's politically correct bullshit that feeds the prevailing fiction—that a movement the majority once reviled as a radical front for communists now belongs as much to them as it does to us, that their roles were as substantive as ours, that it took no more courage for black middle school children to face down the dogs and fire hoses of Jim Crow than it did for grown white men and women born to the privileges of this society.

This is how our history and culture continually slip from our grasp. We allow the majority to interpret our history for us and feed their interpretation back to us through schools they control. That interpretation is inevitably filtered through a White Racial Frame—the same frame they hung around their necks and ours all those centuries ago. Naturally, any such interpretation puts the majority at the forefront. We're relegated to the background because to do that is why the framework was created and why it persists today.

The Movement fought against impossible odds to force the government to acknowledge our civil rights, and we prevailed. The victors supposedly write history, yet the information elite rewrites our history to minimize our central roles within it. I repeat: our history is rewritten to minimize or erase our contributions to it. That's like letting someone steal your identity. The story of how we fought against the organs of mainstream power and won legal recognition of our rights is twisted into a story of mainstream triumph. That story of mainstream triumph is the one we learn in school. Blacks not old enough to have lived through the Movement are just as likely to believe that story as whites.

> *"Americans want to be descendants of a noble people,*
> *explained David Blight, a U.S.-history professor and the*
> *director of Yale's Gilder Lehrman Center for the Study*
> *of Slavery, Resistance, and Abolition. Americans want*
> *to be the people who emancipated the slaves—not the*
> *people who enslaved them."* [11]

Conservatives have taken this perversion of the Movement and King's legacy to its extreme, using snippets from King's "I Have a Dream" speech to paint him as a "colorblind" conservative who stood against the policies he actually promoted. Ronald Reagan, who throughout the 1980s continued to imply that King was a communist, used the "I Have a Dream" quote in 1985 to slam affirmative action.

> *"These people tell us that the Government should enforce discrimination in favor of some groups through hiring quotas, under which people get or lose particular jobs or promotions solely because of their race or sex. . . . Twenty-two years ago Martin Luther King proclaimed his dream of a society rid of discrimination and prejudice, a society where people would be judged on the content of their character, not by the color of their skin. That's the vision our entire administration is committed to."* [12]

Note the assumption of American (i.e., white racial) purity embedded within Reagan's words. He speaks to a nation completely free from any vestiges of racism or prejudice against blacks or any other people—a nation in which no past injustice need be righted, in which there was no blame, no guilt, and no debt because there had never been any wrong. Within Reagan's words, white Americans have been perpetually pure. In the America he fabricates, all have been equal, all have been free. In Reagan's mythical America, no one was robbed of her freedom and belittled and viciously discriminated against for most of this nation's history; that never happened in Reagan's America. His words grew from the deeply entrenched American myths he so ingeniously exploited—those of a nation born pure and perpetually righteous and to which the sight of our black skin puts the lie, reminding as it does of centuries of gross injustice, violent enslavement, and cruel apartheid.

Conservatives, ranging from David Horowitz to Glenn Beck to Rush Limbaugh, have misused that same bit of "I Have a Dream" that Reagan quoted. The right-wing Heritage Foundation even printed a piece by Robert Woodson and William J. Bennett titled "The Conservative Virtues of Dr. Martin Luther King."

Considering all the right-wing misuse of King's words, Paul Rockwell in the *Los Angeles Times* set the record straight with direct quotes from King:

Reporter: "Do you feel it's fair to request a multibillion dollar program of preferential treatment for the Negro, or any other minority?"

Dr. King: "I do indeed. . . . Within common law, we have ample precedents for special compensatory programs. . . . America adopted a policy of special treatment for her millions of veterans. . . . They could negotiate loans from banks to launch businesses. They could receive special points to place them ahead in competition for civil service jobs. . . . There was no appreciable resentment of the preferential treatment being given to the special group.

"A society that has done something special against the Negro for hundreds of years must now do something special for the Negro."[13]

Expounding on the remembrance of King and the Movement he symbolized, Gary Younge, author of *The Speech: The Story Behind Dr. Martin Luther King Jr.'s Dream,* beautifully summarized the mainstream success at neutering King's message:

> *"They can't remember him as the guy who rallied against poverty and called against government intervention because that's still going on. But to remember him as that man who articulated that great moment where America decided to get rid of codified segregation, well he articulated that moment like nobody else had, and that's a very convenient way to remember him.*
>
> *"So part of the reason that the dream is remembered in the way that it is, is because it's a way Americans can forget the rest of the stuff he said."*[14]

The twisting of King's words and legacy happens partly because civil rights education of any kind is sorely lacking in this country. And if civil rights education is lacking, imagine the dearth of education on aspects of our history considered less flattering to the majority.

In his forward to the Southern Poverty Law Center (SPLC) report "Teaching the Movement: The State of Civil Rights Education in the United States 2011," Julian Bond wrote:

> *"I began teaching civil rights history some years ago at some of the nation's most prestigious colleges and*

universities. Fearful that I might be 'speaking down' to my students, I gave them a brief quiz when the first class gathered. The results showed me that my fears were misplaced. None could tell me who George Wallace, the segregationist governor of Alabama, was. One thought he was a CBS newsman who had covered the Vietnam War. They knew sanitized versions of the lives and struggles of Martin Luther King, Jr. and Rosa Parks, but nothing of their real stories. "[15]

The SPLC report graded states on a rigorous set of standards. But even discounting areas that require anything more than a contextual understanding of the Movement, the overwhelming majority of states failed miserably. The standards ask that "Students . . . be able to identify key events in the Civil Rights Movement and place them in the correct chronology," which, considering the state of American history education, probably ain't gonna happen. However, even when you limit the required understanding to a contextual overview of the Movement, its causes, its players, and its breadth, most states still fail. For instance, in the category of understanding opposition to the Movement, which is about as basic as you can get, 38 states rated "0." Another 12 states rated 25%. That means that in the vast majority of states, students learn nothing or next to nothing about the massive opposition to the Civil Rights Movement.

Unfortunately, white students aren't the only ones learning very little in those classrooms. According to the SPLC study, most Afro-American students learn in school that the Civil Rights Movement was a comparatively minor event of Southern regional interest. If the topic is covered, it is cursorily. They learn a sanitized version that subtly supports the white racialist frame on which this country was founded—the Hollywood version of black liberation—that it was largely the doing of good white people, which is an extension and deepening of the "it was an all-American movement" fiction.

The fate of the history of the Civil Rights Movement is indicative of the way our history is regularly distorted or omitted within mainstream contexts born of our racial sub-humanization. Slavery is central to Afro-American history. The majority do all in their power to minimize its significance in theirs. The impact of slavery on American politics is defining, but that's not the lesson in your son's or daughter's junior high school textbook. Nor will it be in the foreseeable future because the majority aren't half so "perfectible" as the popular portrayal of the Civil Rights Movement would have us believe. As so many twist the mantra of "content of their character" by draining it of all context, history is not so ignorable as they would have us believe.

The Civil Rights Movement Was a Political Appetizer to a Cultural Meal That Was Never Served

From its initial marquee campaign—the Montgomery Bus Boycott—to its final successes—the Civil Rights and

Voting Rights Acts, the Civil Rights Movement's aims were political. It sought corrective legislative action and some subsequent means of enforcement. It was not devised to, nor did it ever bill itself as, addressing the legacy of hundreds of years of enslavement and dehumanization on the black American psyche.

With his extraordinary achievements and the towering strength he displayed, Martin Luther King was a man of his time. Born in 1929, he came to maturity in the heady American atmosphere of postwar possibility—when men could literally seek the stars. He sincerely believed in the Christian ethos. He sincerely believed in the perfectibility of mankind.

Armed with the belief in the rule of law and in the majority's belief in the same, the Movement saw politics as a vehicle for advancement. When, even after the judicial and legislative victories of *Brown vs. Board of Education* and the Civil Rights Acts, segregation reigned, the Klan still terrorized, and you could still get beaten senseless for insisting on not being called "Boy," the contract was broken. Black Americans' belief in 'the system' collapsed. Frustration and rage erupted. In 1965 Los Angeles, where 95% of the housing was off limits to blacks due to racist restrictions, the Watts riots erupted.

In seeing politics as a remedy for racist America, the Movement was proven wrong. It won extraordinary political victories, and our rights had to be recognized in law if they were ever going to be recognized in fact. However, the former did not lead to the latter, and we found ourselves in much the same position we had fought so valiantly and restrainedly to overcome.

In seeing politics as a remedy, the Civil Rights Movement never painted us as more than America's political issue, which had been our traditional role born of our early racial categorization. We were a political issue at the founding of the Republic, which the Three-Fifths Compromise proves. That "political problem" role did not accord us the status of human individuals, much less that of a cultural entity or fully formed people.

Through proving our power to battle and sway a reluctant nation, the Movement's gains opened the door for us to see ourselves differently. However, by necessity, the Movement functioned from, even while slashing against, our accepted role as a political bone of contention to be raised up or put down at the majority's whim. For a time, the Movement forced the majority to place us at the fore—long enough to enable landmark civil rights legislation that changed the legal face of the nation. However, the movement did not identify us, to ourselves or other Americans, beyond America's 200-year-old political race "problem." Seeing us brutalized on television elicited sympathy, but seeing puppies similarly treated would have done the same and might have led to puppy anti-brutalization legislation. But it would not have changed the way we regard puppies.

The Movement was of its time, and thus it focused on how the majority saw and treated us. It never had the chance to focus on the need to see *ourselves* differently to effectively ensure our equality or superiority in our own eyes. Because it was, at its core, a political strategy, the Movement put only African-American *political* aims front and center, and those aims demanded that white folks' sensibilities remain paramount, for there could be no political progress without winning them to our political side. The Movement had to sway the majority. The Movement's rhetoric had to often be as much about whites as blacks because it was all about getting the majority to do something—change the law and enforce the law. It was not about our confronting and codifying our legacy in this nation such that we took control of our identity from within and then took the power to radiate that identity to the world.

Toward that end, the Movement was a start—nothing more.

Frustration was an understandable emotional reaction to the trauma Movement activists endured for minimal gains on the ground. People got mad.

Black Power became the rallying cry, *demands* for our rights replaced pleas for the same, and we looked everywhere for an empowering identity. We had the right idea. The Movement allowed us to recognize our power, and we desperately needed to raise ourselves out of that huddled, defensive political crouch to which the double consciousness condemned us.

We looked everywhere for a way to redefine ourselves except in the most obvious place. We looked to Africa as if it were a monolithic entity instead of an outrageously varied stew. We ignored our complete severance from our slave ancestors' homelands. We ignored the inconvenient fact that most of us could just as accurately trace a healthy portion of our ancestry to Scotland as to western Africa. We struck poses in leather with guns. Dashikis and Afros were potent political statements. We shuffled hair, clothes, costumes, and rhetoric to forge an identity outside the one that had left us curled on the ground shielding ourselves from white racists' kicks and spittle and white cops' flailing batons. When it came to redefining ourselves, we were young, like archers peppering every ring with arrows save the bull's-eye.

The activists of the Black Power movement were as naïve as those of the Civil Rights Movement when it came to belief in the human capacity for change and their abilities to foment change in others. If the arc of human progress does, in fact, bend toward justice, it does so at a crippled, confused snail's pace. The "revolutions" that the activists envisioned were, in fact, mere adjustments. The branch on which they pulled with such might did bend, but it snapped back almost as much. White reaction to black demands brought us the Republican Party's "southern strategy," which threw a thin veil of respectability over its racist appeals to white voters.

The Black Power movement devolved into chaos with a healthy assist from the FBI and its counterintelligence program (similar to one less effectively aimed against the mainstream Civil Rights Movement). Subsequent civil rights efforts focused on policy, leaving our identity, as usual, to the mercy of the majority's vision of us, our history, and our culture.

In 1968, writer Cecil Brown wrote of Richard Wright's *Native Son*:

> *"To reject Wright's art is not to reject protest; it is to reject negative protest, to reject the white man's concept of protest, which is that of a raging, ferocious, uncool, demoralized black boy banging on the immaculate door of White Society, begging, not so much for political justice as for his own identity, and in the process, consuming himself, so that in the final analysis, his destiny is at the mercy of the White Man."*[16]

This is an apt description of the favored image of the black male for both blacks and whites in the late 20th century. We had been searching wildly and contorting spasmodically to forge an identity both separate and lofty, but settled for something white folks could stomach—and buy.

He's Your Monster, Not Mine

By Leonce Gaiter
Published in BUZZ Magazine, June/July 1993

Just as the Rodney King civil-rights trial was winding down and Los Angeles was nervously preparing for who-knew-what, I read two articles in one week about "Monster Kody." The first, in *Esquire*, was an excerpt from a soon-to-be published memoir *Monster: The Autobiography of an L.A. Gang Member*. The second, in the Los Angeles Times Magazine, was a prologue to the building media frenzy surrounding Monster, a.k.a. Kody Scott, a 29-year-old African-American former member of South Central's Eight Tray Gangers Crips who came by his nickname after beating another man so brutally that police called it the work of a monster.

The first article was irritating; the second made me sick. Not since I first saw photos of black men and women with their backs disfigured from slave masters' whips, not since I was first called nigger by some ignorant white man, not since I saw an image of a dead African-American man swinging by the neck from a tree while white men, women and children grinned, pointed, and laughed—not since then have I been so convinced that so many white men and women truly hate and wish death upon African-Americans.

Here are the facts: In his book, Monster admits to murdering African-Americans. Monster further admits to beating men nearly to death and to robbing and knifing and stealing. Monster Kody now sits in Pelican Bay State Prison, a maximum-security institution that houses the most violent of the violent, serving seven years for robbery. And there his name and legend would have likely stayed had it not been for a white man named William Broyles, Jr. Broyles, a respected journalist and screenwriter, was not the first member of the white elite to become fascinated with this butcher. Leon Bing, a white former fashion model, had previously written about him in *Do or Die*, her 1991 book on black gangs, which reads like Dian Fossey's memoirs—a helpless white woman among large, hairy, dangerous black gorillas of the African forest, who outwits the beasts and earns their trust. (The whole of Bing's book rests subliminally on a "threat of rape" foundation, a truly sick exercise.) But Broyles didn't want to write *about* Monster; he wanted Monster to write. Kody had, as Broyles put it, "native talent"—an interesting choice of words, a variation on Leon Bing's theme, that pegged this Monster as a *talking* gorilla.

Broyles encouraged the Monster not only to write a book but also, as one would with any other oddity, to put itself on display. (For the jacket of his book, Monster appears shirtless, pumped up, gang tattoos bared, holding a semiautomatic weapon—a black, murdering beast.) One wonders if Broyles would have been as encouraging and nurturing had this been an African-American writer who was his social equal. One can only wonder.

Broyles sent a sample of the Monster's writing to his agent, Lynn Nesbit of the prestigious New York literary agency Janklow & Nesbit. She, to her credit, was less than impressed. But white Terry McDonnell, the editor in chief of *Esquire*, ate it up. So did white Morgan Entrekin of the Atlantic Monthly Press, who called the Monster a "primary voice of the black experience."

Another fascinating choice of words: To me, this is a white man who thinks that a monster who butchers African-Americans is a major voice for all African-Americans, a white man who thinks of all blacks as less than human, as a murderous sub-species. And here is a white man who has decided to publish a book that will prove his thesis to as many readers as possible.

Once white people like Entrekin made the Monster "hot," white Lynn Nesbit put her good sense aside and gave the manuscript to one of her junior agents, Lydia Wills, an ambitious—and white—29-year-old. Wills apparently did her job. So much so that, as Mark Gompertz of Avon Books put it, bidding for the publishing rights to the book took on "a circus atmosphere."

What else? This is the story of a talking gorilla. The selling point was a natural: You know you cringe when you see one walking toward you on the sidewalk. Well, here's why, and in the Monster's OWN WORDS. This is what THEY are really like. IN THEIR OWN WORDS.

"The funny thing is," Broyles told the *Times*, "here's this guy who I'm encouraging to write in pencil from prison, who I talk to on the pay phone with guys yelling in the background, and he ends up making $200,000 or more. It's great." Remember: Kody Scott beat a man so viciously that the police called it the work of a monster. Perhaps that is what caused one British publisher to say of Kody, "Getting that close to evil is *very* interesting," as if he were commenting on the coming fashion season.

Do you believe that only Monsters behind bars can write well? Don't you believe that others, like Ishmael Reed or Darryl Pinckney, might deserve some of the attention lavished on the incarcerated Monsters? Why do you think they receive so little attention? Why do you think that books by black women that vilify black men, published by white-owned-and-operated publishing houses, are so popular? And who do you think decides what will and will not get published and promoted? It's obviously been decided that you *will* read the Monster.

Why? There is no conspiracy here, just ignorant, racist minds at work. I am an African-American man, and I have killed no one. My parents worked, educated themselves, and raised their children. I graduated from Harvard. My sisters hold advanced degrees. *This* is the black experience.

Each step of the way, a roadblock or two was put in my parents' paths, and in mine. We overcame them. *That* is the black experience. Maya Angelou's voice rings as loudly as did Thurgood Marshall's. *That* is the black experience.

Yet a group of white men and women would have you think that Monster Kody speaks for me, for my family, for my African-American friends. Our stories they would find uninteresting, I'm sure.

Early in this century, a Pygmy man was placed in a cage and put on display in a freak show. They do it differently now.

Develop the Tools to Resist the White Racial Frame, or Molder Within It

The "White Racial Frame" is a concept developed by sociologist Joe Feagin after decades of research on racism.

> *"Fostered constantly by white elites through the institutions of cultural transmission—academia and faith communities, political discourse and media—and reinforced by a majority of white parents and peers, the contemporary white racial frame is deep and pervasive, with numerous sub-frames. . . .*
>
> *"This dominant frame shapes our thinking and action in everyday life situations. Where and when whites find it appropriate, they consciously or unconsciously use this frame in accenting the privileges and virtues of whiteness and in evaluating and relating to Americans of color."*[17]

It is critical to understand that mainstream views of our history, the culture formed from that history, and the goals of our liberation struggles are all usually presented through the lens of the White Racial Frame. This is what I believe Afro-American historical and cultural self-education must counter—and from a very young age. We have been taught that the view through that white Frame is more glorious than any other. Thus, we are tempted to accept the fictions and images that it propagates. When we accept the Frame, we get to cheer certain aspects of America along with our white countrymen, not realizing that we denigrate ourselves and our triumphs in the process. When we accept the Frame, we lose ourselves in a "feel good" aura that Frame exudes due to its familiarity and seeming "rightness." It feels "right" to focus on the roles whites played in the Civil Rights Movement, doesn't it? It feels inclusive, which we must always be; it proves that blacks aren't "holding a grudge" or hurling blanket accusations of racism at our countrymen. Note that no such prerequisites appear when whites discuss World War II, for instance. Must black soldiers' efforts be highlighted to prove that whites are free from racism? When the Founders are mentioned, must one also mention their enshrinement of slavery in their documents of freedom and democracy? No. It's different for us, though. The White Racial Frame insists that Afro-Americans consistently prove our Americanness through acts of contrition. We must, when discussing our history, regularly absolve the majority for their race-based sins, thus proving our American bona fides and reinforcing the foundations of that very same White Racial Frame, which are:

- An "accented view of *white virtue* [that] overrides the actual reality of racist performances."

- Strong sense of personal and group entitlement to what whites have—with an underlying assumption that this is fair—while willfully ignoring (intentionally forgetting, remaining "invincibly ignorant" of) the horrific history and the ongoing injustices that, in fact, produce these things.

- A denial of racism's magnitude and impact that operates from the assumption that the white experience is the universal experience.[18]

Sound familiar? These are the girders of modern conservatism and the jet fuel of Donald Trump's election victory. Gazing through the White Racial Frame leads the majority to see our history as theirs and their history as ours. A glaring example is the prevalence of the "White Savior" concept of Afro-American history. The White Savior lets the majority portray themselves as ever righteous—in keeping with treasured American myths—regardless of historical facts.

In the popular book and film *The Help*, a virtuous young white woman gives black maids their voice in 1963

Mississippi. The piece presents white racist characters in the pre–civil rights South as aberrant monsters, not normal, average people, when in fact, in 1963, 68.7% of University of Alabama students agreed with one of the following statements:

- Some Negroes may be just as capable, intelligent . . . as the white man, but this is the exception.

- American Negroes do not have the capacity to compete with white students in white universities.

- I have never met a Negro who is my equal in intelligence.

The White Savior is prominent in films from *Django Unchained* to *Dangerous Minds* to the *The Blind Side* to *Amistad.* In each movie, whites hand blacks the power to overcome barriers and injustice; we never take it for ourselves. This reinforces the Reaganesque/Trumpian frame of perennial white virtue, which bleeds into the insistence on highlighting King's mentions of "brotherhood" and whites' roles in the Movement (black history through a White Racial Frame), while ignoring King's calls for white racial self-examination and correction, affirmative action to right historical injustice, and recognition of an America still teetering on a white supremacist foundation (black history through an Afro-American lens).

Why should we be at the mercy of the majority's conception of our great liberation struggle or any other aspect of our history and culture? As the majority cherry-pick our history to promote its narrative, why don't we use the fullness of that history to promote our own—to each other—from childhood onward? Why don't we paint our struggles and triumphs to form a complete picture, thus promoting pride in ourselves and our accomplishments, instead of expecting the majority to present our past in any light other than the most self-congratulatory for them though that may prove deprecating to us?

That is why the argument that "black history is American history" is naïve. American history, as it is overwhelmingly taught and understood, does not do justice to Afro-American history, and Afro-American history does not belong to the mainstream to do with as it pleases; it is ours. Do we want to continue to teach our children our history through a White Racial Frame, for that is the practical effect of saying "black history is American history"? First, it puts historical and cultural education of our youth in the hands of the majority. It states that we must wait for the majority to finally "come around," shed all vestiges of prejudice, and magically acknowledge the history they've been loathe to seriously regard for over 100 years. It then states that the majority veil should be placed on the history that we teach our children. It states that we should forgo the right that every other culture assumes—the right to teach our history from our own point of view, to be the principals of our own stories—and, instead, subsume our history within the majority's. It states that we do not have the right to express our rage at the barbarities we endured, for those are histories that the majority have little willingness to accept and examine, and for good reason: it puts the lie to treasured American myths.

Afro-Americans, as a people, do not systematically teach our young our own culture and our own past. We relegate that role to public schools and thus to a majority that have historically despised us. It is as if Jews allowed Christian Europeans to teach them their culture. The idea is unimaginable. Yet that's the position in which Afro-Americans find ourselves. American school systems will never adequately educate Afro-American children in their own culture any more than they will adequately educate Native Americans in their tribal traditions. Why, you may ask, should these groups need specific cultural education when those of Italian or Greek or Hungarian descent do not? Because this country was founded, quite literally, on the dehumanization and slavery of kidnapped Africans. It was built on the dehumanization and genocide of native peoples. No other groups in America have had their very humanity destroyed as an integral part of the rise of this nation. These are the cruel facts. And when a nation is built on your bones and blood, it leaves a wound. When for hundreds of years your status as fully human is denied by every organ of the State, the majority and their culture absorb that idea of your status—and pass it back to you. When that happens, such cultural self-education becomes necessary.

This is our great cultural challenge. Every culture has the obligation to use its history to its own advantage. The only excuse for our not doing so is that we have so internalized this nation's hatred toward us that we have failed to recognize ourselves as a cultural entity and force worthy of organized self-study.

The Civil Rights Movement focused on politics, and the Black Power Movement was so drunk on image that it too often ignored our very American historical and cultural substance. Neither took as its charge to recast this nation's history into our own. They never got to the point of ignoring the warped mirror that the majority hold up, reflecting their warped image of both us and them. We never held up our own mirror, full of our own images of us (and yes, them) based on the self-taught facts of our tragic and triumphant sojourn in this country. We never traveled back to this nation's founding to teach ourselves this America through our own eyes as clearly and decisively as the majority have taught it through theirs.

I Will Happily Disembowel
Whoever Next Says "But We
Elected a Black President"

"Post-racial began to come into vogue after Obama won the Iowa caucuses and fared well in the New Hampshire primary.

"The Economist called it a post-racial triumph and wrote that Obama seemed to embody the hope that America could transcends [sic] its divisions."[19]

During the presidential election of 2008, a media brouhaha arose regarding whether Barack Obama was "really black." It was indicative of our lack of Afro-American cultural consciousness. That lack represented a major reason we failed to understand the cultural complexities of Obama's elevation to the presidency and why we allowed and sometimes participated in the nonsensical "post-racial" meme that became the latest incarnation of the White Racial Frame. Our lack of cultural consciousness and subsequent inability to educate the media and the majority are partly to blame for so many Americans seeing Obama's presidency as a post-racial proof point: They would support a black man; thus, they bore no prejudice. Racism was over; whites now had proof that they were as pure as they had always insisted they were within the White Racial Frame.

Of course, Obama was just as black as any other black person. However, Obama was not just any black man. We failed to understand that Obama was a political one in a million. He was a demographic and racial three-headed chicken, a sociopolitical freak. He was the American majority's Holy Grail of black men.

One of the principal, unacknowledged factors in Barack Obama's successful rise to the presidency was the fact that he was NOT born to Afro-American *culture*. He adopted it in young adulthood. His father was African, not Afro-American, African—not an American descendant of African slaves. Obama's mother was white. He was, in fact, principally raised and nurtured in mainstream American culture, largely by his white Kansan grandparents. Nothing in his background attached him to America's great crime. He was not raised with the casual, laughing stories of how much food his great aunt had to cook before taking a two-day road trip because the restaurants were segregated and she knew none would serve her on the road. His father did not tell him of the beating he took the first time he tried to register to vote.

He did not witness his father's fury when recalling the fact that, as a black man, he could not find a place to live after returning from fighting this country's wars. He did not hear tell of how the local preacher and undertaker offered advice whenever local blacks had to negotiate unfamiliar white bureaucracies. He did not experience a close-knit, self-reliant black society either directly or vicariously through elders. Through them, he did not understand the pain this country's racism caused them.

In short, Barack Obama neither represented nor reflected to the majority the taint of America's historical viciousness toward the American descendants of African slaves. Born to an African man and a white woman, raised by whites, his exposure to that history during his formative years was comparatively minimal.

I was not raised in a household with white parental figures. However, I have lived my life in principally white environments outside of the home, and I can assure you that Obama's conceptions of race under the tutelage of his white mother and grandparents were extraordinarily different from mine—even with my mega-immersion in the mainstream. Obama having lived his formative years free from Afro-American cultural norms—having been raised with no intimate, firsthand testimonial knowledge of this country's treatment of us—allowed him to speak to a national white audience in terms that they did not find threatening to themselves or to their ideal of themselves as righteous and historically innocent. He did not have to disturb their comfortable, white frame of reference. Not having been raised Afro-American, his history bore nothing to discomfit them; he had been raised just as they had. His forebears had not endured America's unique forms of dehumanization, torture, and terrorism aimed at Afro-Americans.

In fact, the moments when the facts of Afro-American history entered his campaign were among its most troubled. When the Reverend Jeremiah Wright gave vivid voice to Afro-American rage, Obama had to distance himself.

When Michelle Obama, born to Afro-America, said at a Wisconsin event "for the first time in my adult lifetime, I'm really proud of my country," the conservative right tried to paint her as a radical Black Panther Gurl, a position clumsily mocked on an infamous *New Yorker* cover.

Born in 1964, Michelle Obama was old enough to absorb this country's reaction to the civil rights and other rights movements. Through her Afro-American parents and family, she doubtless accessed the history this country often seems so desperate to forget. There is nothing so unusual about a woman from a historically despised population reserving her national pride for a moment when the nation seemed poised to act in a way that belied its hate-filled history. Imagine an East German Christian clergyman saying at the fall of the Berlin Wall "for the first time, I'm really proud of my country." Americans would have applauded him and championed the quote as an acknowledgment of the cruel Soviet-era realities and the possibility of a new dawn. However, when

Michelle Obama "got real," as they say, John Podhoretz in *Commentary* magazine wrote:

> *"Can it really be there has not been a moment during that time when she felt proud of her country? Forget matters like the victory in the Cold War; how about only things that have made liberals proud—all the accomplishments of inclusion? How about the passage of the Civil Rights Act of 1991? Or Ruth Bader Ginsburg's elevation to the Supreme Court? Or Carol Moseley Braun's election to the Senate in 1998? How about the merely humanitarian, like this country's startling generosity to the victims of the tsunami? I'm sure commenters can think of hundreds more landmarks of this sort. Didn't she even get a twinge from, say, the Olympics?"*

He suggests that an Afro-American woman should get the same level of pride from athletes' performances in the Olympics as she does when a majority of voting Americans seem poised to do the historically unthinkable—elect a black president—one whose skin looks like hers—skin that a relatively short time ago could have gotten him beaten or killed for so much as *approaching* a local ballot box. Ditto the selection of a female to sit on the Supreme Court or a single state's election of a black female senator. None involve the attitudes and habits of a vast swath of American adults. None involve stature and majesty in remotely similar ways. None were unthinkable within the African-American community in similar ways.

Could anything better display his worldview's ignorance of or disregard for her history and her culture?

Large swaths of white American voters managed to overcome Barack Obama's skin color. This was easier to do for him than it would have been for almost any other black man because with Obama, skin color was an end in itself and represented little (and in Afro-American cultural terms, nothing) of this country's historical crimes. There was no indigenous subcultural baggage attached to his skin. Yes, the majority have historically reacted to the black, but it's easier to see past it when there are no pools of blood and piles of broken bones behind it. Because his father was not American, his mother was white, and white men and women raised him, Barack Obama could speak of his American story without even tangentially indicting America (more on this later). Ninety-nine percent of Afro-Americans cannot do that without soul-crushing contortions. This does not diminish his extraordinary accomplishment in navigating America's racial minefield and ascending to America's highest political office. It simply means that his road there was unique. His ascension was not, nor can it be, a template that most of us can follow. We have neither the parents nor the past for that. Nor did his ascension signal a sudden transformation in the American mainstream's regard for Afro-Americans. We are still more likely to be stopped by police for no reason, less likely to get a job than identically qualified whites, or more likely to die from preventable causes.

What Obama's election did signal is what a sense of cultural entitlement can do. It signaled what assurance of your worth and knowledge of your rightful place can get you. We cannot mimic anyone's heredity and upbringing. But we can use our American cultural journey to ground our claim to everything this country has to offer, as opposed to defending ourselves against the majority's cultural contempt. We can use our culture to acknowledge, counter, and free ourselves from the defensive crouch of reacting to the White Racial Frame and, instead, offensively stake our rightful claim to everything our talents merit. This is the power Obama's white grandparents instilled in him; he was raised with none of the historically born "can't haves" that are passed on like mother's milk to most Afro-Americans.

To date, we have allowed the majority to dictate the terms on which we view ourselves and our place in this country. That doesn't have to be—not if we finally embrace our past and all that it has robbed us of, and all that we have bought with it, and use both to build the scaffold on which all of us can stand and look down upon the American landscape below, saying all the while "this is mine—as much or more so than it is any other American's." To do this means upending the lessons the mainstream has insisted we take from our own history, triumphs, tragedies, and great liberation struggle. It means claiming ownership of the facts of who we are and how we got here and doing the hard work of teaching them to one another, generation after generation, as close to the cradle as we can.

No. Barack Obama's political triumph did not "disappear" racism any more than Martin Luther King's did. In both instances, many were so desperate to forget what little of our past they still acknowledged, so desperate to reinforce the American myth of Godly perfection, that they elevated the men and their achievements to redeem themselves on the cheap. Instead, Obama was raised solely in the mainstream culture by white parental figures without any of the historically race-based negatives that history has beaten into most of us. He then adopted Afro-American culture in young adulthood, and not having been raised in the negative glare of the majority's warped mirror, he saw power and strength in that culture sufficient to help, against all odds, propel him to the nation's highest office. The greatest lesson we can take from him is to ensure that those of us raised within the culture pull from it that same strength.

A Somewhat More Visible Man

By Leonce Gaiter
Published in *The Huffington Post*, December 5, 2008

I've often wondered what it might mean to "feel" American—to truly accept its glories and shame as my own. Looking at and listening to the Cindy McCains, George W. Bushes and Ronald Reagans of the world, I've wondered. The country they describe bears so little resemblance to the one in which I've lived, very different from the one in which my parents were raised. When they speak of American moral supremacy, of unsullied American justice and righteousness, of the deathless wisdom of the Founders, I cringe. Such statements omit me. For 188 of this nation's 232 year history it was legal in America for a white man to first own or destroy my black life at will; and subsequently, it was legal to erase me and those like me from the mainstream of social, economic, and political life. This latter was apartheid, as deadly and vicious as that ugly word implies.

Yet, we speak of an unsullied America, an America somehow free from sin, a past and perpetual shining city on the hill for all men and women. That is a lie. My parents' lives prove it is a lie, as did theirs before them. And yes, as their offspring, I prove it is a lie. It is my duty as their offspring to remind America that it is a lie. I owe it to them and what they sacrificed to remind us all that the McCains and Bushes and Reagans continue the tradition of omitting the sons and daughters of African slaves. I owe it to my forebears to remember that this perfect, mythical country is one where my past is quashed—psychologically deleted . . . one in which I am deleted. In this mythical, exceptional land, I am the blight that must be forgotten. I am its version of the shunned Victorian madwoman prone to blurt the family's filthy secrets, locked in an attic to keep them hidden. The secrets slowly poison everything beneath the capacious manor roof, but the residents suffer the rot and stench to maintain their precious image of upright sanctimony.

Barack Obama, the half-black son of a Kenyan and a Kansan—and unmistakably "black" man who has unwaveringly adopted Afro-American culture, has just been elected President of the United States. Some will say that this proves American racism is dead. Some, like the Reagans and the Bushes and their political brethren, have been saying that for decades, and it remains transparently ignorant and self-serving. Countless tales from this election alone prove the point. There is ample research to prove that we have neither outgrown our American cultural history nor our animal distrust of those who don't look like us.

No, this election does not mean the end of American prejudice, bias, racialism or racism. Job applicants with black-sounding names will still be 50% less likely to get a given job than those with less distinctive tags. However, the election does have deep meaning, particularly to me, and I'll be so bold as to suggest that I may speak for many other blacks as well. I am not trying to belittle the satisfaction that whites might feel at this sign of progress—their own progress. However, such satisfaction is only personal if one overcame a conscious distaste for blacks in order to push the "Obama" button. If not, the satisfaction is second-hand; it's an easy kumbaya moment. It costs nothing emotionally. It demands that you neither acknowledge an altered reality about yourself, nor adjust any long-held belief.

I have often wondered what it meant to feel fully American. Today, I received my first glimpse. I have no illusions. I know that the country's catastrophic state bears as much credit for the Obama victory as his rational, intelligent response to it, and his skillful, disciplined campaign. Nonetheless, it is heartening to think that issues can trump our ugly racial scars—that we can stop picking at the scabs long enough to consider our own self-interest above our historical prejudice. Considering from whence we've come, that is huge. Think of all the blood that has been shed to get here. Hundreds of thousands died on U.S. soil to preserve the right to keep me in literal chains—to own me like you'd own a dog. Sociologists Steward E. Tolnay and E.M. Beck identified:

"2805 [documented] victims of lynch mobs killed between 1882 and 1930 in ten southern states. Although mobs murdered almost 300 white men and women, the vast majority—almost 2,500—of lynch victims were African-American. Of these black victims, 94 percent died in the hands of white lynch mobs. The scale of this carnage means that, on the average, a black man, woman, or child was murdered nearly once a week, every week, between 1882 and 1930 by a hate-driven white mob."

Untold numbers died from neglect, substandard, segregated medical care. Millions went uneducated and locked away from opportunity. Four little girls died when a white man bombed their church. Three civil rights workers, one black and two Jewish, were murdered because some white men hated us unto death. White assassins' bullets murdered Medgar Evers and Martin Luther King. This is a small sampling. Millions died in slave holds on the way to this country. The list goes on.

Some white Americans rail against such litanies. They call it living in the past, or insist that the past is insignificant. They can speak so foolishly because, in general, white Americans just don't do the past. They don't have to. And they don't understand those who do. It's at the root of many of our international failings. Many American memories don't extend beyond their own lifetimes. We don't understand that most of the world lives the past each and every day. Unlike the majority, black Americans live the past every day. We have no choice. We are its children. Southerners often live the past. War was fought in their backyards, and they lost. Americans have an uncanny ability to jettison the past with each generation. You can do that when you don't have to look, every day, at scars it left behind.

I have often wondered what it meant to feel American, and today I have the glimpse because a black man, who is half-white, wears a sense of entitlement unsullied by any of the "can't-haves" that history has carved into black psyches in the course of the American past. Raised by white women and men, he seems to have a sense that he did not have to snatch or steal his due from America, but that it was his for the taking. His most primal human relationship—with a mother—was with a white woman. He watched those who loved him—his grandparents—make disparaging remarks about those who happened to look like him. Confusion ensued, and led to his throwing in his cultural lot with the descendants of African slaves. However, his acceptance was "academic" if you will. It was learned, not lived. And in learning as opposed to living it, he did not have to absorb the degree of fear and suspicion that the rest of us inherit. Just the opposite; his white family and formative years in brown-skinned environments probably helped inure him to such fear and suspicion.

I remember as a young child in school in the late 60s and 70s hearing how in America, anyone can grow up to be President, and knowing that it was a lie, knowing that if America had the balls to bet her glory on that statement, America would lose. If any American could grow up to be President, and I could not (men died in the streets to secure my right to merely vote) then I did not qualify as American.

Rivers of black blood have been spilled. My parents and theirs fought and died to rip their rights from the majority's avaricious grasp. To justify their illegal hold, the majority belittled, dehumanized, brutalized and sometimes killed me and mine. So I have often wondered what it might mean to feel fully American. Today, I, a black descendant of African slaves, get a glimpse, and it feels good. I get a glimpse because the white part of a half-black man raised by whites who adopted black culture allowed him to see a different country from the one my history has burned into my mind. In America's long, perverse history of race relations, such absurdist irony is fitting.

PROGRAMMED FOR PREJUDICE: THE BIASED NORM AND WHY WE MUST PREPARE FOR IT

In today's 21st-century post–civil-rights-era America:

- Blacks and whites use drugs at about the same rate; thus, adjusting for population, five times as many whites are using drugs as African-Americans, yet African-Americans are sent to prison for drug offenses at 10 times the rate of whites.[20]

- African-Americans represent 12% of the total population of drug users but 38% of those arrested for drug offenses and 59% of those in state prisons for a drug offense.[21]

- "African Americans serve almost as much time in federal prison for a drug offense as whites do for a violent offense."[22]

- *"The researchers at the University of North Carolina-Chapel Hill analyzed more than 1.3 million traffic stops and searches by Charlotte-Mecklenburg police officers for a 12-year period beginning in 2002, when the state began requiring police to collect such statistics. In their analysis of the data, collected and made public by the state's Department of Justice, the researchers found that black drivers, despite making up less than one-third of the city's driving population, were twice as likely to be subject to traffic stops and searches as whites."*[23]

They found that blacks were much more likely to be pulled over for minor infractions, such as seat belts, registration, or equipment—offenses that officers may cite at their discretion—while whites were most often pulled over for safety violations, such as speeding and running stop signs (i.e., blacks were stopped more when the cops had a choice—when cops wanted to; whites were stopped principally when the cops had no choice—when public safety was at risk).[24]

- *"Between 2011 and 2013, the Grand Rapids Police Department either cited or arrested approximately 560 people for trespassing on business property, pursuant to the trespassing-letter policy. In a city in which black people make up roughly 20 percent of the population, 59 percent of those detained for trespassing under this policy were black. Perhaps even more telling is the fact that African-Americans are more than twice as likely as whites to be arrested, rather than simply ticketed, when the police bring charges for trespassing on the property of an open business in Grand Rapids. . . .*

Under a policy similar to Grand Rapids' No Trespass Letters . . . [o]ne African-American man was stopped more than 250 times for suspected trespassing on the property of the convenience store where he worked. More than 60 of those stops resulted in his arrest." [25]

- A team of Harvard researchers found that black boys faced harsher punishment because they're often perceived as older than they actually are.

  "[That] study also involved 264 mostly white, female undergraduate students from large public U.S. universities. In one experiment, students rated the innocence of people ranging from infants to 25-year-olds who were black, white or an unidentified race. The students judged children up to 9 years old as equally innocent regardless of race, but considered black children significantly less innocent than other children in every age group beginning at age 10, the researchers found."

  "The students overestimated the age of blacks by an average of 4.5 years and found them more culpable than whites or Latinos, particularly when the boys were matched with serious crimes, the study found." [26]

- In 2012, the Department of Education Office for Civil Rights found that the Christina School District in Delaware had violated Title VI of the 1964 Civil Rights Act.

  "'Our investigation identified examples where African American students engaging in virtually identical behavior to white students were punished more harshly than white students (who had the same or worse disciplinary history),' the department wrote in a letter to the district. 'A statistical analysis of all students referred for discipline for the first time, based on the District's own records and categorizations, found that African Americans were at least twice as likely to receive a suspension . . . than white students for violations of similar severity. Moreover, African Americans experiencing their first referral were over three times more likely than white students to have the suspension be [out of school] rather than [in school]. For students whose first disciplinary referral was for Inappropriate Behavior, African American students were nearly seven times more likely to receive [an out-of-school suspension] than white students.'" [27]

We have been waiting for our 50-year-old political triumphs to trickle down (or up) such that the majority acknowledge and battle flagrant injustice against us. In most instances, that has not happened. Whether the disparities catalogued above are the result of race hatred or subconscious bias simply does not matter. What does matter is the effect on black lives. Everything else is noise. Racist outcomes are hateful. How you get to hateful is of little interest. When you take up residence at hateful, as opposed to gunning it out of that toxic neighborhood, your motives cease to matter. When you consistently support policies that result in racist outcomes, you are racist.

In too many areas, America has parked at hateful. From all evidence, a significant portion of the majority is comfortable there. There is nothing exalted about the human propensity for prejudice toward those who don't look like us—and make no doubt that it is an ugly, animal, human propensity that infects all of us. White skin does not render one immune, although it often seems to provoke a brutal case of denial.

We have been waiting a long time for the majority to "come around" and attain the colorblind state to which they claim we should all aspire, a status to which many believe the Civil Rights Movement elevated them.

We have been waiting in vain.

We Are Bigots All

Psychologists Drs. Mahzarin R. Banaji and Anthony G. Greenwald of Harvard and University of Washington, respectively, are among the many researchers who have demonstrated the lie of "colorblindness," or the belief that prejudice is a rarity or an aberration. Banaji and Greenwald developed Implicit Association Tests (IAT) that reveal unconscious biases against various groups, such as blacks and women. In the introduction to their book, *Blindspot: Hidden Biases of Good People*, the authors state:

> *"In this book we aim to make clear why many scientists, ourselves very much included, now recognize hidden-bias blindspots as fully believable because of the sheer weight of scientific evidence that demands this conclusion. But convincing readers of this is no simple challenge. How can we show the existence of something in our own minds of which we remain completely unaware."*[28]

The race IAT (the only one I'll be discussing here) considers how we equate black faces with weapons and danger.

> *"The belief that Black men are criminals persists even though the likelihood of any given Black male being a criminal is low. Needless to say, the existence of a stereotype associating a given group with violence and crime is grave and has important implications for the individual, group, and society."*

An academic understatement. If white police officers think that every time a black man reaches for his pocket, he's reaching for a gun, they will shoot black men more often. And they do. A ProPublica analysis of killings by police showed that young black males were 21 times more likely to be shot by a police officer than young white ones.[29]

The race IAT first asks takers to self-report their association of blacks with weapons. This "self-reported" aspect of the test asks whether you acknowledge explicit bias. Next, comes the "automatic" part of the test, meant to uncover unacknowledged or "automatic" bias. You're asked to match individual images of one of four categories (black faces, white faces, weapons, or harmless objects) with one of two labels "weapons or African American faces" or "harmless objects or European American faces." The test then turns the tables, asking you to match individual images of those same four categories with "weapons or European American faces" or "harmless objects or African American faces."

It sounds complex, and it is. You're first asked to label objects as "harmless" or as "weapons." Harmless objects included things like soda cans and cell phones. Next, you label faces as "African American" or "European American." Once accustomed to that, you are asked to associate, for instance, a soda can with one of two labels: "weapon or African American" or "harmless object or European American."

"As data from many respondents show, 70 percent or more of the people to take this test have greater difficulty with sheet B, which pairs White with weapons, than with Sheet A, which pairs Black with weapons. Analyses of more than eighty thousand race-weapons IATs completed at implicit.harvard.edu yielded three important results:

"First, the automatic Black = weapons association is much stronger among all groups who took the test— White, Asian, Hispanic, and even African American— than is suggested by surveys that asked questions about this association. Second, the size of this automatic stereo- type varies noticeably by groups—it is largest in Whites and Asians, next largest in Hispanics, and smallest in African Americans. **But even African Americans show a modest Black = weapons stereotype** *[emphasis mine].*

"Third, comparing results of the two kinds of tests— reflective self-report and automatic stereotype—reveals another interesting fact about who carries the stereotype. The higher the education level, the lower the endorse- ment of the association between Blacks and weapons on the reflective self-report answers. However, on the test of automatic stereotypes, the IAT, education level mat- ters not a whit. Those with the greatest education carry as strong an implicit Black = weapons stereotype as do those with the least education."

It didn't matter that test takers stated that they held no animus toward blacks. A majority still *displayed* bias toward blacks in the automatic portion of the test. The research- ers call this "unconscious" bias. (I suspect a not-insignifi- cant percentage of this is less unconscious than it is simply unconfessed; however, that might be my bias talking.)

It didn't matter how well educated the subjects were. They still displayed bias against black faces, more readily associating them with weapons and violence.

Not only that, but studies also show that bias and preference form early. By around age 5, racial preferences begin to show themselves based on a child's natural propensity to favor those who look like him or her—a propensity that is then reinforced by social cues and hardens into open negativity toward black faces surprisingly early. (Interestingly, the study found that young children chose to befriend a black child with a native accent before a white one with a foreign accent. It seems language can trump race in the "hatestakes.")

One study seeking to determine when infants graduated to race-based preference tested how readily children aged 10 months, 2.5 years, and 5 years exchanged toys with other-race individuals. In the first two tests, the youngest children exchanged toys as readily with same-race individuals as with other-race individuals. The 5-year-olds, however, "expressed explicit social preferences for own-race individuals."[30]

Other studies came to similar conclusions. One study, titled "The Development of Implicit Attitudes: Evidence of Race Evaluations from Ages 6 and 10 and Adulthood," found that not only does racial bias appear around age 5 but that children even acknowledge it around that age:

> *"Remarkably, implicit pro-White/anti-Black bias was evident even in the [6-year-olds], with self-reported attitudes revealing bias in the same direction. In 10-year-olds and adults, the same magnitude of implicit race bias was observed, although self-reported race attitudes*

*became substantially less biased in older children and
vanished entirely in adults, who self-reported equally
favorable attitudes toward Whites and Blacks.* [31]

In other words, the 5-year-olds have not yet learned to lie
about their bias. By age 10, however, they have, and they
declare themselves less biased than tests show them to be.
By the time they're adults, the lie of "colorblindness" is
complete. Adults report themselves freer from bias than
tests show them to be.

A 2010 study commissioned by CNN found that
5-year-old "white children have an overwhelming bias
toward white and that black children also have a bias
toward white but not nearly as strong as the bias shown
by the white children."

*"A 5-year-old girl in Georgia is being asked a series of
questions in her school library. The girl, who is white, is
looking at pictures of five cartoons of girls, all identical
except for skin color ranging from light to dark.*

*"When asked who the smart child is, she points to a
light-skinned doll.*

*When asked who the mean child is she points to a
dark-skinned doll. She says a white child is good because
'I think she looks like me,' and says the black child is
ugly because 'she's a lot darker.'"* [32]

That's by age 5. Add to that a couple more decades of
negative imagery and inference of blacks as dangerous,

ignorant, and inferior, and what do you get? You get the average American adult. You get a bullet train for blacks from preschool expulsions to the penitentiary; you get bias in housing and hiring, lending and policing, health care and legal protections.

It's imperative to reiterate that black children also displayed antiblack bias—just less so than white children. This phenomenon was first signaled when, in the 1940s, Afro-American psychologists Kenneth and Mamie Clarke conducted now-famous experiments using dolls to assess the impact of racism and segregation on the self-esteem of black children aged 3 to 9. The dolls were identical in all aspects except skin and hair color: some were black with brown hair, and some white and blond.

The questions were designed to determine children's preferences, knowledge of racial differences, and self-identification with racial groups:

> *"The results of the Clark and Clark (1947) study revealed that 67% of Black children preferred to play with White dolls, 59% chose the White doll as the nice doll, and 60% chose the White doll as having a nice color. Additionally, 59% chose the Black doll as being the one that 'looks bad.' Interestingly, overall only 58% of Black children selected the Black doll as the one that 'looks like you.'"* [33]

Now, back to the 2010 CNN study:

> *"The tests showed that white children, as a whole, responded with a high rate of what researchers call 'white bias,' identifying the color of their own skin with positive attributes and darker skin with negative attributes. . . .* **[E]ven black children, as a whole, have some bias toward whiteness, but far less than white children** *[emphasis mine]."*[34]

A 2013 paper for the *Journal for Social Action in Counseling and Psychology* acknowledged a wealth of studies buttressing the IAT work and doll studies addressed above and went further to cite some sources of the displayed bias:

> *"More than fifty years after the original Clark and Clark study, researchers conducted a version of the doll experiment using cartoon characters. African American and White preschool children showed a trend toward selecting White cartoon characters as their 'best friend' instead of the African American characters (Jordan & Hernandez-Reif, 2009). The enduring findings of doll studies (Banks, 1976; Byrd, 2012; Cross, 1985; Gray-Little & Halfdahl, 2000) are seen as indicative of messages in American society that devalue African Americans. These messages are transmitted early in the lives of African American children despite all of the gains of the civil*

rights movement, the growth of the African American middle class and the election of the first American Black president (Veroni-Paccher, 2012)." [35]

I was tempted to call the next citation one of the most "shocking," but it isn't. It's not shocking at all. The lure to use "shocking" was my societal training whispering like a devil in my ear. To call it "shocking" would suggest that I think better of my fellow Americans than the citation suggests I should. Declaring myself shocked would mean that I am neither cynical nor jaded. But the finding does *not* surprise me. I have lived in this country all my life— among the white majority all my life—and it does not surprise me. It is therefore not shocking. It is, however, something else. It is *disgusting*.

"Historical representations explicitly depicting Blacks as apelike have largely disappeared in the United States, yet a mental association between Blacks and apes remains. Here, the authors demonstrate that U.S. citizens implicitly associate Blacks and apes. In a series of laboratory studies, the authors reveal how this association influences study participants' basic cognitive processes and significantly alters their judgments in criminal justice contexts. Specifically, this Black-ape association alters visual perception and attention, and it increases endorsement of violence against Black suspects. In an archival study of actual criminal cases, the authors show that news articles written about Blacks who are

convicted of capital crimes are more likely to contain ape-relevant language than news articles written about White convicts. Moreover, those who are implicitly portrayed as more apelike in these articles are more likely to be executed by the state than those who are not.[36]

The research, conducted over six years at Stanford and Penn State, used principally white, male undergraduates. The researchers "primed" their subjects with black or white male faces flashed on a screen for a fraction of a second. "Researchers found subjects could identify blurry ape drawings much faster after they were primed with black faces than with white faces."

"The researchers consistently discovered a black-ape association even if the young adults said they knew nothing about its historical connotations. The connection was made only with African American faces; the paper's third study failed to find an ape association with other non-white groups, such as Asians. Despite such race-specific findings, the researchers stressed that dehumanization and animal imagery have been used for centuries to justify violence against many oppressed groups."[37]

In discussing their work, the researchers point to the fact that the iconic "march of progress" evolutionary illustrations almost invariably "progress" from ape to white man—presenting the latter as the pinnacle of evolutionary achievement.

Figure 8 – Typical chart tracing evolution
from chimpanzee to (white) man

These researchers also looked at the practical implications of this dehumanization. They primed their subjects with words associated with apes, such as "monkey" or "gorilla," or with words associated with big cats, such as "lion" or "panther." The cat words were used as a control since they also suggest Africa and violence. The students were then shown a video clip of police violently beating a man "of indeterminate race." However, a mugshot of a black or white man was shown prior to the clip to indicate who was being beaten.

"Participants who believed the suspect was white were no more likely to condone the beating when they were primed with either ape or big cat words, Eberhardt said. But those who thought the suspect was black were more likely to justify the beating if they had been primed with ape words than with big cat words."[38]

What are the results of this dehumanizing link?

> *"This link has devastating consequences for African Americans because it 'alters visual perception and attention, and it increases endorsement of violence against black suspects.' For example, the paper's sixth study showed that in hundreds of news stories from 1979 to 1999 in the Philadelphia Inquirer, African Americans convicted of capital crimes were about four times more likely than whites convicted of capital crimes to be described with ape-relevant language, such as 'barbaric,' 'beast,' 'brute,' 'savage' and 'wild.' 'Those who are implicitly portrayed as more ape-like in these articles are more likely to be executed by the state than those who are not,' the researchers write."*[39]

These messages and attitudes do not exist in intellectual or social vacuums. They have influenced policy and helped to keep blacks poorer and less educated than the majority.

* * *

I often see the Rogers and Hammerstein lyric from the musical *South Pacific* cited by those professing or promoting universal brotherhood:

> *You've got to be taught to hate and fear*
> *You've got to be taught from year to year*
> *It's got to be drummed in your dear little ear*
> *You've got to be carefully taught*

This is only half true. You may have to program active hatred into a child, but bias comes preloaded. It's part of the human software package. As human beings—as the animals we are—we naturally lean toward in-group bias. To suggest that one is "colorblind" is to suggest that he or she has ascended beyond the merely human. Are these "colorblind" Americans really the next evolutionary leap? That would be the only explanation for their extra-human egalitarian sensibilities.

A tendency to prejudice alone does not make a person bad. It makes him or her a person. Period. A bad person is one who *denies* that he or she is just as prone to prejudice as any other human. A bad person is one so convinced of his own semigodliness that he insists he's free from bias, so no thought or action of his could be based thereon. Having declared himself preternaturally pure of heart and thought, he has permission to act on those prejudices without guilt or shame—and lets them thicken into the pustule of racism . . . lets them congeal into actions that actively harm other people. Consider the human propensity toward prejudice akin to our natural need to defecate. Toddlers do it where they sit. We work hard to teach them to do otherwise to avoid the smell and the mess. As Americans, we blithely walk around with steaming pant loads of bigoted offal, all the while pretending we don't smell a thing.

This is why Afro-Americans need systematic cultural self-education from as early an age as possible. We need to learn the animal sources that buttress the American history of the prejudice we encounter so we don't accept that bigotry as our truth. We need lessons that allow us to instantly counter the negativity toward us when it occurs, as opposed to believing it as the studies above show we often do.

Martin Luther King said, "We must learn to live together as brothers or perish together as fools." The critical word in that sentence is "learn," and it's what many in the majority have shown too little interest in doing. They took their willingness to "allow" us our civil rights as both absolution and amnesia pill. It was neither. It was a toe in the water of ridding this nation of its hateful baggage. The majority dipped their toes, and many declared themselves not only fully immersed but also newly baptized. In many ways, we acted as if we believed them by taking no steps beyond the political and the cosmetic to slough off the toxic blanket America had thrown over us and thus secure and advance our place in this society.

In America, with its enduring racist history and subsequent investment in antiblack bias, you have to be carefully and specifically taught *not* to be prejudiced against African-Americans in general and Afro-Americans in particular. That's teaching for which the majority are not clamoring, many holding the delusion that it's unnecessary, which grows from their notions of white supremacy, which feed prejudice . . . *ad infinitum.*

History is not over. It walks beside us every day. This nation's racist history did not disappear with the passage of the Civil Rights Act nor the Voting Rights Act nor the election of Barack Obama. Pre-Trump, overtly racist speech and actions were often tsk-tsked in a way they were not in the past, but this only invokes the famous Malcolm X quote, "You don't stick a knife in a man's back nine inches and then pull it out six inches and say you're making progress." Post-Trump, overtly racist speech and actions are making a stunning comeback, with attempts to ban an entire religious group from entering the country, the appointment of a white nationalist as a White House advisor, and the elevation to Attorney General of a man once deemed too racist to be a federal judge. With the elevation of Donald Trump and his tacit endorsement and normalization of overt American race hatred, even the prior tsk-tsking may go the way of the dodo.

In America, we have magnified the natural intergroup prejudice to which humans are prone by a history in which a nation grew fat on Afro-American labor while befouling every value it claimed to hold dear to keep us enslaved and then subjugated. To maintain its belief in its ideals of freedom, equality, and justice while simultaneously disregarding them, this nation had to make us less than human. All men could still be equal, but only if black ones were less than men. Thus, we were reduced to subhuman status and every legal and social mechanism in this country worked to keep us there. This nation's economic strength and elevated self-image depended upon it. In fact, the majority came to define themselves solely in opposition to us. They defined themselves as 'white.'

Fear of White, or "There Is No Spoon"

A 2013 study published in the National Communication Association's journal, *Communication Education*, explored black students' fears that they would lose their cultural identity while attending majority white colleges.

As a product of largely white neighborhoods and elementary, middle, and secondary schools, white universities and white workplaces, I have felt this fear. I understand it. However, I also find it counterproductive and indicative of a narrow and self-limiting definition of our cultural identity—one still reeking of our initial racist classification and subsequent immersion in its negatives.

In a synopsis of the study's findings, Dr. Shawn T. Wahl of Missouri State University wrote:

> *"A specific struggle that emerged from the data was a battle within the African-American student between her or his 'blackness' and the perceived 'whiteness' of his or her university. The dialectical pull occurred within the subjects as they struggled to be proud of themselves and*

their 'blackness,' and at the same time, they struggled to learn and adapt to the 'whiteness' of their schools."[40]

He quoted one subject as saying:

"There is a war going on inside of me between my blackness and your whiteness. When I see myself in the mirror, I see a competent, talented black woman. Then I go to class, look around, and realize that I need more. My blackness seems too . . . um . . . black, like I need to be more than who I am, I need what you [as a white person] have. I need an understanding of how things work, you know, politically. My blackness, my personhood isn't enough. I need to whiten myself to succeed."[41]

She is wrong. The 'whiteness' she sees as separate and apart, is, in fact, an integral part of her 'blackness.' This is a fundamental statement of Afro-American existence, articulated in 1903 by W.E.B. Du Bois:

"The history of the American Negro is the history of this strife,—this longing to attain self-conscious manhood, to merge his double self into a better and truer self. In this merging he wishes neither of the older selves to be lost. He would not Africanize America, for America has too much to teach the world and Africa. He would not bleach his Negro soul in a flood of white Americanism, for he knows that Negro blood has a message for the

world. He simply wishes to make it possible for a man to be both a Negro and an American, without being cursed and spit upon by his fellows, without having the doors of Opportunity closed roughly in his face."

In fact, it is the girl's 'blackness' to which her white counterparts have no access. It is they who are lacking, not her. Again, everything within the mainstream (or 'white' world)—save its historical contempt for the 'black'—is as much ours as any other American's. We contributed as much to enabling it as they.

That an 18+-year-old Afro-American student has not yet reconciled the fundamental duality of her cultural identity is worrisome. Because she was never provided the tools to master her existence as an Afro-American in a white-dominated society with white supremacist foundations, she finds herself adrift in young adulthood when confronted by the majority. Thus, along with the challenges of looming adulthood, collegiate self-exploration, and getting grades, she has to struggle with racial positioning issues that might have been acknowledged, if not addressed, many years earlier.

In 1960, 60% of black college students attended a historically black institution. That number is now just 20%. Today, most black students attend mainstream universities. Clearly, for many of these students, college is their first immersion in that mainstream. For many, segregated housing, neighborhoods, and schools have ensured limited personal exposure to it.

"There is a war going on inside of me between my blackness and your whiteness," the student declared. What is "your whiteness" and how does it threaten "my blackness"? As stated, every aspect of 'white' culture is mine, and I am black. There is no 'whiteness,' save its historical contempt for the black. In the film *The Matrix*, the protagonist watches a child bend a solid spoon with his mind, and in explaining the method, the child says, "Do not try to bend the spoon. That's impossible. Instead, only try to realize the truth. . . . There is no spoon."

There is no 'white' world. There is only one to which you, as an Afro-American, have not yet laid your rightful claim.

We can't try to inhabit or displace 'white culture' because there is no white culture, save a history of hatred and violence to which no sane person would wish to lay claim. There is a Russian, a Jewish, an Italian, a Scottish, and a German culture, but there is no 'white culture.' In the United States, there is only American culture, inherently polyglot and mulatto. It is ours as much as theirs— and we are black (and you can say the same of brown, tan, red, and yellow). It is our Afro-American culture to which *they* have little exposure or access. In donning the 'white' mantel of privilege all those years ago to hoard America's riches and deny us access to them, 'white' became no more than an oppositional negative. It had (and has) no meaning except that of a private key code to the American kitty, much of its treasure looted from us. Since so many Americans jettisoned their original cultures (English, Irish, etc.) in favor of the privileges of becoming White Americans, the empty 'white' is now the only identity they have. Some are desperate to keep it shackled to "American" so that one feeds the other. White conservatives, the self-appointed keepers of traditional white American identity and all of its negatives, said Obama was Kenyan, that he was un-American, that he hated America. They said that because Obama as president threatened that once unassailable bond between whiteness and full American identity. A black man in the highest office of the land—a black American president who openly identified with Afro-American culture—that was a bald challenge to white supremacy and thus to white identity.

Why is this student seeing the mainstream culture in opposition to her own, as opposed to seeing it *as* her own? Yes, her own Afro-American culture will alter how she owns the mainstream, but it does not preclude her from doing so. To cede American culture—the mainstream— 'white' culture (call it what you will)—to "them," when we are, and have always been, central to it is self-eliminating. It is an acceptance of a white supremacist frame.

At a Whitney Museum event, Michelle Obama put the same point in more personal terms:

"You see, there are so many kids in this country who look at places like museums and concert halls and other cultural centers and they think to themselves, well, that's not a place for me, for someone who looks like me, for

someone who comes from my neighborhood. In fact, I guarantee you that right now, there are kids living less than a mile from here who would never in a million years dream that they would be welcome in this museum.

"And growing up on the South Side of Chicago, I was one of those kids myself. So I know that feeling of not belonging in a place like this. And today, as first lady, I know how that feeling limits the horizons of far too many of our young people."

I repeat: Mainstream America and its culture are ours as well because, at various levels and in various forms, we eat and drink it from birth alongside every white man and woman. Throughout American history, we have informed it as much as any. The only aspect of mainstream culture that should be out of reach for us is its disdain for us and ours.

Statements from various students in the Missouri State study show a longing for the "easier" all-black worlds of their precollege days. One stated, "I grew up in an all-black neighborhood and school. I had never seen so many white people in a classroom before. Suddenly, I was the minority and I did not feel comfortable speaking out in class."

In fact, the student was not "suddenly a minority"; segregation had made him unaware that he always had been. This is America, and blacks are a small part of the population. Of course, for many, entire histories of racist municipal policies, real estate contracts, and lending practices have left blacks ghettoized in all-black worlds, with their attempts to explore beyond their confines retarded and diminished by policies that target those who look "out of place" (i.e., black) in principally white environments.

Another student in the study stated, "The only time I am asked to speak is if an issue about slavery or the ghettos enters the realm of the conversation. I wasn't around for slavery. I don't live in a ghetto. I have other thoughts, but they don't seem important to anyone else. So why bother to talk at all?"

Who waits for an invitation to speak? If asked to speak on the topic of ghettos with which you have no familiarity, ask why the questioner would assume you had firsthand knowledge of the subject. If there are topics on which you have something to say, speak out. Don't wait for white folks to invite you to do so. Your life is not a dinner party at their manor house. There are no codes governing your behavior beyond those that constrict everyone else. We are not guests in their world. This world is ours—all of it. But we'll never learn this if we lack the opportunity to experience them and the mainstream world they inhabit up close and personal. "Stop and frisk" and "broken windows" policing are little more than excuses to harass blacks who fail to stay in their proverbial and literal places. We don't need to make their work any easier by denying ourselves as well. The more time we spend with the mainstream, the less foreign it becomes, and the more we are able to navigate and utilize it to our own benefit. With lack of access, the mystique grows, and with that mystique grows the intimidation and fear that this student expressed.

Call this "the resilient mystique of whiteness." I had an aunt who was born in the mid 1920s. One dinner-table conversation lodged itself permanently in my mind. She had been raised in a small bayou town outside of Baton Rouge, Louisiana. She was discussing her work and mentioned that she had disagreed with a superior, told him that he was wrong, and provided the proof to back it up. She then proclaimed proudly, "And I said that to a white man."

This conversation took place in the early 1970s and shows how this black woman, raised during the height of American apartheid and white terror, took pride in the strides she'd made toward overcoming her fear of whites and their world. Aren't these students' expressions of fear of losing themselves and tales of intimidation unto silence just different aspects of my aunt's stifled fear? It's a vision of whiteness as mysteriously powerful and dangerous. Look out, it says, or the white will steal your blackness; speak out of turn, and it will harm you. I believe this is a logical extension of the fear we've carried throughout American history for our very physical safety in principally white environments (a fear still often rational today). To profess fear for your blackness or cultural heritage is far more face saving than admitting fear of the mainstream and your ability to function within it. This is why I believe that integration at the school or neighborhood level is crucial for us. My aunt had been raised in the segregated South. One generation later, I at a young age, was sufficiently surprised at her expression of pride at "talking back" to a white man that it stuck in my head as an oddity. That was the difference between a terrorized, segregated upbringing and one in which I interacted with whites as equal, superior, subordinate, and everything in between. It's essential that black children play, fight, and compete with white ones. We have to challenge them, beat them, and lose to them. I know from experience that this removes any mystique from them or the culture that some of them still dare to claim as theirs alone.

I realize that when school districts go through pains to resegregate, there might be little Afro-American citizens can do about it. That is when you do the next best thing: take advantage of their absence and teach these segregated children through an Afro-American lens. Let them learn why they are isolated, the history from which it stems, the gall of those clinging to vicious histories who would deny their due. Then encourage them to storm the citadels of the mainstream to claim their rightful share of it.

In her extraordinary and incredibly disturbing 1979 novel, *Kindred*, writer Octavia Butler creates a world in which a modern black woman named Dana is inexplicably and repeatedly transported back in time to 1815, where she confronts a slave society and the white man named Rufus who will father her direct forebears. She is brutalized physically and psychologically, but she cannot retaliate against Rufus because to kill him or let him die before he fathers offspring will destroy her not-yet-born self. To read the book is to seethe and even wish that the protagonist would simply kill the monsters who treat her and those like her so savagely. But even as you rage, you realize that it is her own life she is saving and those of the children she may have and their children. In the end, after her ancestors are born and safely free, Dana does finally kill Rufus when he tries to rape her. However, by that time, such damage has been done that the victory is unspeakably costly.

The book posits a ruthlessly complex world in which a black woman's very existence as a being on this earth depends upon the continued existence and even the safety of a white man who would sell her as chattel and brutalize and rape her.

Similarly, all of Afro-America is the product of such men. The historically racist America is our Rufus. And like Dana, we have paid an enormous price for our continued existence. Through developing our own view of ourselves, our history and culture, and teaching each subsequent generation, we can finally, metaphorically, kill the savage who would have us seen as "less."

Country to Call My Own

By Leonce Gaiter
***Washington Post*, July 1997**

Like so many other black men of his generation, my father was raised in a small Southern town. He grew up wandering the fields of rural Louisiana and swimming in the local bayous. He talked constantly about that land. He loved it. And he tried, through his stories, to spark some love for it in me.

But, along with the tales of swimming in the muddy creeks and stealing fruit from neighbor's orchards, there were tales of burnings and beatings at the hands of local whites. While wanting me to love that land as much as he did, my father inadvertently taught me to despise it. Who could love a land that bred the horrors he described, that he'd lived through? I cursed the place he loved so dearly.

I don't remember specific lessons. No one sat me down and told me, "fear what's beyond the city's boundaries. They're like dogs out there. They'll tear at you, for no reason other than that's what they are." The fear and contempt for the rural was just passed down, often inadvertently, as if part of the African-American cultural ether. I learned to beware what lay beyond this line or that. White folks lived there, and they could be killers.

I remember driving with my family in the late 1960s from one Southern military posting to another, and seeing one of those "Welcome To . . ." signs that greeted you along the highway as you entered a small town. The signs were sometimes elaborate billboards plastered with round insignia of Elks' Clubs and Kiwanis and the United Brotherhoods of this and that. The billboard I most remember had a dedication on it. It said, "The Knights of the Ku Klux Klan welcome you to . . ." I was about 9 years old at the time. This enormous state-sanctioned billboard, blaring the town's hatred for blacks, only confirmed that rural America did not welcome people like me.

I feared and hated more than just "them," though. To me, it was also what they controlled that threatened me—the very air they breathed and the land they walked upon. After all, those elements had bred and nurtured them. They must have borne the sickness within them as deeply.

I grew to feel, as many other black Americans do, that we were safe in our urban enclaves and just about nowhere else. The greatest black urban migration occurred a mere 50 years ago, but for hundreds of years we'd been concentrated and subjugated in the rural South. The land was a reminder of where we'd been, of the opportunities we'd been denied, of the bowing and scraping we'd been forced to do. To reject the land was to reject that legacy of subservience and downtroddenness.

Young blacks like me learned to belittle what the majority and our own cultural memory kept from us. Perhaps we belittled the land so we wouldn't feel that sting of denial so keenly. I scoffed the peace and beauties nature offers. They were fictions.

That has changed for me. I recently moved from Los Angeles to a rural Northern California town called Paradise in the foothills of the Sierra Nevadas. I had spent my adult life in large cities—Boston, Washington, Los Angeles, New York—and, like so many people, black and white, the ills of the megalopolis had become too glaring to me, too physically and emotionally draining to be borne any longer. One of the lucky ones, I could ply my writer's trade anywhere. So I left.

According to census statistics, black Americans have been moving back to the south in record numbers. Census officials predict that this return to the south will continue into the next century. Along with the repatriation of the South, there is a greater willingness for black Americans to live in rural settings, shedding the "urban" tag we'd carried for so long, which we'd both internalized, and had hung upon us from without.

I had visited Paradise several times in the past few years. Its sharpness stunned me. Set among the tall Ponderosa pines, the air was so fresh that it almost stung when you sucked it in, and its modest homes nestled in the shade and covered in fallen leaves looked more charming and homey than their arrangement of wood and brick could justify.

I found myself lying by a stream, hearing nothing but the wind in the leaves and the water flashing by. I felt my shoulders settle down from up around my ears where they'd been perched for the past several years, and I knew I would have to make such a place my home. Finally, I'd gained some understanding of what my father tried to tell me all those years ago.

I watched this town's white faces with care, gauging reactions to my black self. I noticed none. And for the first time in my life, I had felt that real progress had been made in this country, because even if some of these rural folk still had contempt in their blood, most had learned not to show it. And that was all I demanded of them.

All parts of this country have their racist legacies, and this town is no exception. Former residents tell tales of the sheriff from the days long gone who swore he would shoot any "nigger" who dared come into town. Even before I officially moved here, my "worst" fears were realized: While I was walking in town one morning, a pickup sped by and some local put his head out the window to yell "nigger" at me.

I'd hoped that such a scene would never occur. I had thought that such ugliness would sour this place for me, that its natural beauty would be snatched away from me once more, just as I was learning to bask in it. That's why I dreaded hearing that word.

But I supposed I'd grown old and ornery enough not to care, not more than I had to, not any more than the implied threat in that word insisted I care (the "prepare to fight and defend yourself" that that word calls up). It just meant that the threat to black folks lived here too—just as it does in the big city. But I can live with it. I'd outgrown my civil rights-era vision of a United States in which no such threat exists. Such threats have always been, and always will be, a part of being an American for me.

These white men and women were no longer the rural goblins of my father's past and my imaginings. They no longer held that status.

Throughout the 1970s there was a great deal of talk about black "liberation," but too much seemed just talk. It wore the bravado of those not quite convinced of what they were saying. It is a true sign of emotional liberation that we will no longer allow ourselves to be denied any single place in this country that we, more than just about any other group of citizens, have the right to call our own.

I was raised by a man who grew up in the bayous of Louisiana. I spent my young life in cities where my father sought and got a better life than his old country town would allow him. I spent my young adulthood loathing the land and the people that forced my father cityward. And now, approaching middle age, and on my own terms, I find myself floating on back—back to the trees and the streams and the land.

INTERNALIZATION

". . .internalized racial oppression [is] defined as the individual inculcation of the racist stereotypes, values, images, and ideologies perpetuated by the White dominant society about one's racial group, leading to feelings of self-doubt, disgust, and disrespect for one's race and/or oneself.

Like all forms of internalized domination, internalized racism is not the result of some cultural or biological characteristic of the subjugated. Nor is it the consequence of any weakness, ignorance, inferiority, psychological defect, gullibility, or other shortcoming of the oppressed. . . . It cannot be reduced to one form or assumed to affect similarly located individuals or groups in precisely the same way. It is an inevitable condition of all structures of oppression.[42]

I n his 2001 book, *Toms, Coons, Mulattoes, Mammies, and Bucks,* Donald Bogle looked at black depictions in American film and identified these five in the title as archetypical—roles in which the white majority were willing and able to see us. These images comforted the majority and helped them justify and legitimize their malignant behavior toward us. We were either shiftless, ignorant, prey, victims, servants, or oversexualized and rapacious. Such people are not ones you would expect to treat as equals or to whom you should extend basic human rights. These are caricatures, not humans. They deserve neither rights, respect, nor consideration.

Hollywood had codified mainstream views of Afro-Americans, and Bogle broke the code. Hollywood has always been excellent at identifying what its principal audience wants to see. Old Hollywood was also a prime cheerleader for The American Way, presenting relentlessly positive images of the American people as virtuous, plucky, freedom loving, fair, and kind. Black images in Hollywood films were no less considered than the messages of Frank Capra's *Mr. Smith Goes to Washington* or the typical Western.

> *"All systems of oppression not thoroughly coerced through brute force and overt repression involve the dominant group's ability to win consent of the oppressed. . . . The dominant group controls the construction of reality through the production of ideologies or 'knowledge'. . . that circulate throughout society where they inform social norms, organizational practices, bureaucratic procedures, and commonsense knowledge. In this way*

the interests of the oppressors are presented as reflecting everyone's best interests, thereby getting oppressed groups to accept the dominant group's interests as their own and minimize conflict."[43]

To link back to an earlier topic, an example of this is pretending the Civil Rights Movement was as much about white people as it was about us. Through no fault of our own, we largely came to accept the mainstream view of ourselves and accommodate the majority's view of themselves. We learned "our place," and while many chafed and fought, many others counseled "go along to get along." We idealized light skin and straight hair. We referred to each other as "Nigger," a word so historically fraught and toxic that even when used in camaraderie it suggests a brotherhood not just of the downtrodden, but the defeated.

As with all oppressed peoples, we internalized the hatred aimed at us. Not only is this a natural outgrowth of prejudice, but when you're the minority, it is the only voice you're willingly granted. Look, for instance, at black literature. The jewels of our canon are tales of prejudice turned inward to the point of self-destruction. The protagonist of *Invisible Man* literally drops down a manhole and disappears. In *Beloved*, the heroine kills her children to shield them from slavery. In *Native Son*, Bigger Thomas lets his impotent rage propel him to places he does not want to go. These are books by extraordinarily powerful writers. However, I can't help but wonder if books of equal merit in which black men and women overtly sought vengeance for crimes done against them would have been as universally acclaimed. These novels paint us as implosive and thus harmless versus painting us as willfully explosive as any wronged white person would be in similar circumstances.

> *"In fact, we can begin to talk about internalized oppression at the moment that the oppressed accept the identities imposed on them by oppressors. The creation of a dominant, 'superior' class depends upon the existence of groups of exploitable 'others' distinguished by their alleged inferiority."*[44]

It is important to define "internalized oppression" beyond just "I hate myself and they're better than I am and boy do I wish I were white" mantras. Acceptance of the White Racial Frame is a form of internalized oppression because it sustains our dehumanization. To accept America's historical myths is to deny our own historical reality and thus to denigrate ourselves. To accept any man's or woman's insistence, of any color, that he or she is "colorblind" is to deny the value of the heritage my color implies. If you don't see my color and the culture it implies, you are not seeing me. In that case, you're not "colorblind"; you're just blind or plain stupid.

Only modes of being grounded in antiblack prejudice or racial animus can rightfully be called 'white.' To suggest that the 'white' is anything more than a rough descriptor of skin color, to suggest that it represents any identifiable aspect of America outside of its historical race hatred, is to deny our roles in this nation's evolution. It is to constrict our being to roles most likely informed by the contempt aimed at us for so long.

Acceding to the fiction of Martin Luther King as a harmless Uncle Remus figure is to internalize prejudice because that fiction exists only within a White Racial Frame. To deny the fury that fueled the Civil Rights Movement right alongside the insistence on nonviolence is ignorant and dehumanizing. To do so is to perpetuate the images, chains, and stereotypes to which the majority have tried to limit us throughout most of this nation's history.

In America, Jesus Was a White Man

When I was growing up, many of my aunts and uncles had pictures of Jesus on their walls. I vaguely recall one with a somewhat dusky hue to his skin, but the others were white and blond—typical of mainstream Jesus images to this day. Ditto the images in the Baptist churches they attended. The Jesus images were those of white men.

At the Catholic churches associated with the Catholic schools I attended, the Jesus figures on the walls, in the stained glass, and carved on the crucifix were all unmistakably Aryan in aspect. Seek historical Western representations of Jesus, and you will find paintings and drawings of white men. After all, every culture worships gods that look like them—that hold them most dear. Shiva looks Indian. Thor looks Norwegian. Legba looks African. In the West, Jesus looks white.

Cultures nurture their own gods. You might say that we create gods in our own images. In the Christian ethos, Jesus is the Son of God—the direct offspring of the almighty deity. And in American Christianity, that offspring has historically been presented as a very white man. Few black folks give birth to blond-haired, blue-eyed babies. If the Son of God is white, doesn't that indicate the race of his Father? If God and his son Jesus are white and humans are created in God's image, where does that leave black men and women? Does that make us inherently less human than those white creatures in God's own image?

Throughout most of our history, the black church has been the third strand braided between our enslavement and our liberation. While Southerners often introduced Christianity to make us more obedient slaves, the practice soon produced an independence of thought and action liberating in and of itself. The liberating aspects of our take on Christianity are extremely well documented and overwhelmingly accepted. However, because it shines a negative light on mainstream Christianity and suggests lingering negative effects of our religious descent from it, the most crippling aspects of our embrace of the Methodist/Baptist Christian tradition have been too long ignored.

The most crippling aspect of that descent is that in America, Jesus is a white man. Period. The vast majority of the images of Christ that a black child sees in his or her lifetime will depict a person who looks like those who enslaved his forebears and regarded them as subhuman. That black child sees depicted as Lord someone who looks like those who legally denied his rights through the middle of the 20th century. This is a God who not only does not look like him but looks like those who reviled him.

In a 2014 article, a writer recalled seeing images of white Jesus in black churches as recently as the mid-1990s. Christians can protest that Jesus has no color, but that's just sophistry. The religion's own tenets—a flesh-and-blood human savior born of the deity—obviate that possibility. Christianity says that Jesus walked the earth, that he was a man. The New Testament makes little mention of his appearance, but he had one. He looked like someone. Being the dominant group in the West, whites portrayed Jesus as looking like them. No Western individual escapes that image. Protestations of "colorless" Jesus and a smattering of tawny, nappy-haired Christs do not—yet—fully counter the fact that, here and throughout our cultural history, Jesus has been a white man, like God his father. To be blunt, we have worshiped as God one who looks like our oppressors. How much of our willingness to rely on the majority's extra-human perfectibility and simultaneous hesitance to steep our youth in the truths of American racial history can be traced back to that?

And yes, that was the whole point in converting us to Christianity.

* * *

Christianization of slaves boomed during the First Great Awakening, a movement that changed the face of American Christianity. Prior to the Awakening, 18th-century Calvinism had been an intellectualized religious experience, consisting largely of textual study, solemn prayer, and equally somber song. It assumed that there was a huge, unbridgeable gulf between God and his creatures. According to Wake Forest University professor Terry Matthews, "the result was an emphasis on man and his morality, with religion becoming more rational and less emotional."[45]

The Great Awakening changed that by placing religious observance into a more visceral, emotional plane, away from its heretofore intellectual resting place. For instance, clergyman Jonathan Edwards, who had been known for his earnest and intense but nontheatrical delivery, "began to experience a harvest of conversions that were accompanied by exaggerated behavior. People would bark, shout, and run when they were converted."[46] Obviously, this was a much more emotionally vivid religious experience than traditional Calvinism provided.

"At the turn of the 19th century, this new revivalism swept through the south, spreading the gospel of personal salvation through revival meetings. 'Methodist and Baptist denominations experienced a surge of membership, often at the expense of other denominations.' This new revivalism relied more on the power of individual preachers than on established churches, and prompted a 'stark emotionalism, disorder, extremism and crudeness

that accompanied expressions of the faith fed by the ordinary people.'"[47]

Southern slaves became the focus of conversion within this Awakening atmosphere of raw religious emotionalism and direct experience with the divine. These new Methodist and Baptist preachers sought to Christianize this large base. Their direct, emotional appeal was particularly suited to the task. According to historian Albert Raboteau:

"While the Anglican clergyman tended to be didactic and moralistic, the Methodist or Baptist exhorter visualized and personalized the drama of sin and salvation, of damnation and election. The Anglican usually taught the slaves the Ten Commandments, the Apostles' Creed and the Lord's Prayer; the revivalist preacher helped them to feel the weight of sin, to imagine the threats of hell, and to accept Christ as their only Savior. The enthusiasm of the camp meeting, as excessive as it seemed to some churchmen, was triggered by the personal, emotional appeal of the preacher and supported by the common response of members of his congregation."[48]

Initially, some preachers emphasized biblical tales of liberation to best enrapture their enslaved audiences. However, attempted slave rebellions led by Gabriel Prosser in 1800 and Virginia slave Denmark Vesey (whose 1822 attempt at revolution was ironically prompted by the closing of his African church on the grounds that it spread literacy and thus rebellion) panicked slaveholders and led them to severely restrict slave religious practices.

> *"Proslavery advocates posited a solution to these problems by arguing that Christianity would make better slaves; indeed, it would serve as a means of control and docility. To avoid educating their slaves, they would teach only certain parts of the catechism and the Bible orally. The basis of this catechism, among other things, would include certain passages from the Pauline corpus . . . , the curse of Ham, and fostering among the enslaved an otherworldly eschatology (that is, if they were faithful and accepted their lot in life, they would be rewarded in the next life)."* [49]

From this point onward, Southern black religiosity would occur under watchful white eyes. The Christian faith was now more fully subservient to the Southern status quo.

> *"Religion became a mechanism of social control, which was particularly important in the middle and southern colonies where Africans represented a larger, more vital work force."* [50]

So we have two important forces at work: slave conversions were dominated by the direct, emotional Methodist/ Baptist evangelism of the Awakenings that minimized the rational in favor of the visceral, and slave worship became subject to a great degree of white control despite black attempts to worship in secret. By the beginning of the 19th century, the strange braid of African-American Christianity was clearly established: a liberating impulse entwined with an enslaving overtone. Noah's Curse, or the curse of Ham, central to slave Christian teachings, was a major part of the latter. From the Book of Genesis 9:20-27:

20 And Noah began to be an husbandman, and he planted a vineyard:

21 And he drank of the wine, and was drunken; and he was uncovered within his tent.

22 And Ham, the father of Canaan, saw the nakedness of his father, and told his two brethren without.

23 And Shem and Japheth took a garment, and laid it upon both their shoulders, and went backward, and covered the nakedness of their father; and their faces were backward, and they saw not their father's nakedness.

24 And Noah awoke from his wine, and knew what his younger son had done unto him.

25 And he said, Cursed be Canaan; a servant of servants shall he be unto his brethren.

26 And he said, Blessed be the LORD God of Shem; and Canaan shall be his servant.

27 God shall enlarge Japheth, and he shall dwell in the tents of Shem; and Canaan shall be his servant.

Note that nothing in this passage states or even remotely suggests skin color; however, from the medieval age onward, this passage has been read to mean that dark-skinned people were the result of a curse from God for licentious behavior.

"In western Europe, prior to the modern period, the curse was invoked to explain the origins of slavery, the provenance of black skin, and the exile of Hamites to the less wholesome regions of the earth."[51]

Here, it's important to state the obvious: slaves were taught to worship a white Savior in the form of Jesus. There was no doubt about that. The available images presented Jesus as unambiguously white, and there was the assumption that God, his Father, shared his Son's pigmentation. Noah's Curse was an accepted tenet of the Methodist/Baptist Christianity to which slaves were converted, and it insisted that God held dark-skinned people in contempt.

Of course, black abolitionists, such as Frederick Douglass and David Walker, railed against what Douglass called "the slaveholding religion of this land" that had "no possible reference to Christianity proper."[52] Some black preachers also raged against it. However, the influence of Noah's Curse remained so pervasive that it appears in Zora Neale Hurston's 1927 play, *The First One*, and in James Baldwin's 1953 *Go Tell It on the Mountain*. The idea of a white God bestowing Noah's Curse did not disappear with emancipation nor with the independence of the black church.

"Probably the most exhaustive study of 'the Hamitic race' by a black preacher was published in 1937 by Alonzo Potter Burges Holly. . . . In God and the Negro, . . . Holly declared that 'God Almighty has shown, through-out the Bible Record, a peculiar interest in His people of Hamitic Descent.' Holly affirmed the Canaanite ances-try of the Negro and a curse of limited duration but insisted that a perennial malediction would 'run coun-ter to the plan of redemption'"[53]

Slaves were ingeniously converted to a fundamentalist, emotive religion that eschewed critical examination and taught them to worship as gods those who looked like their masters. The religion taught that they themselves were cursed in God's eyes and therefore owed obedience and fealty to white men. It is extraordinary that even in the face of these obscenities, many blacks quickly refo-cused their religiosity to emphasize the possibilities for liberation. The Free Africa Society, the precursor to the African Methodist Episcopal church, was established in 1787 by ex-slaves "as a mutual aid society to address the full range of the needs of African Americans that were not addressed in the regular church gatherings and social opportunities of Philadelphia."[54] However, even as one marvels at blacks' abilities to mold Christianity to suit their ends and the interpretive skill and ingenuity with which they approached Scripture, one must consider the lingering, toxic effects of worshipping a God who looked like those who had considered them so beneath human dignity that they merited enslavement. "Slaves were taught from both Testaments of the bible that the God who created them had made them to be the perpetual servants of God's superior white children."[55] While blacks subtly rejected worshipping a racist God via their own secret services and their own churches, they openly accepted the premise that God allowed their enslavement so that they could gain the benefits of Christian salvation. We openly accepted our lot as accursed of the God we worshipped.

In 1875, Bishop Henry McNeal Turner of the African Methodist Episcopal Church claimed:

> *"God, seeing the African stand in need of civilization, sanctioned for a while the slave trade—not that it was in harmony with his fundamental laws for one man to rule another, nor did God ever contemplate that the Negro was to be reduced to the status of a vassal, but as a subject for moral and intellectual culture. So God winked . . . at the institution of slavery."*[56]

Even in the midst of sometimes rejecting a racist God and using Christianity to promote liberation, a seed of self-loathing remained—the idea of blacks as "uncivilized" lesser beings in need of the white savior. In significant ways, the church reinforced the subhuman racial categorization that the acceptance of the designation 'white' was designed to impose upon us.

In the morning when I rise
In the morning when I rise
In the morning when I rise
Give me Jesus
You can have all this world,
Give me Jesus

The suggestion of the traditional black spiritual's lyrics is that Jesus was more important than "all this world." One may assume that freedom was part of that all-inclusive. Jesus was a satisfactory substitute. To this day, black Christianity maintains the idea that we suffer on earth in exchange for heavenly reward. White-imposed Christianity primed us to accept, and even embrace, suffering and oppression. Our own religious leaders teach the Christian ideal of redemptive suffering as personified in the form of Jesus. We suffer here; we gain salvation in heaven.

A people cursed by God deserve to suffer. It becomes a vicious circle. We are cursed and thus oppressed. We go to church to seek relief from the resulting sorrow. The church tells us it's good to be oppressed and down-trodden. We rejoice in the future reward our misery is purchasing.

Cold, empty bed, springs hard as lead
Pains in my head, feel like old Ned
What did I do to be so black and blue?

No joys for me, no company
Even the mouse ran from my house
All my life through I've been so black and blue
How sad I am, each day I feel worse
My mark of Ham seems to be a curse, oh

How will it end? Ain't got a friend
My only sin is my skin
What did I do to be so black and blue?

—ANDY RAZAF, FATS WALLER, HARRY
BROOKS, "BLACK AND BLUE," 1929

The idea of predestined misery, of blackness as curse, is so ingrained that it expresses itself in the popular culture and in our folklore. In her book *Mules and Men*, Zora Neale Hurston quotes a black folk tale she called "Why Negroes Are Black," which ends "So God hollered 'Git back! Git back!' And they misunderstood Him and thought He said 'Git black,' and they been black ever since." This puts us somewhere between God's mistake and our own.

Even in Africa, where blacks represent the overwhelming majority, it has required an active campaign to divest Christianity of its racist, colonialist taint. Part of this drive has been to connect Christianity to native African religiosity. Another has been to tie Christianity to African liberation. This puts Jesus into the native African roles of "Mediator," "Witch Doctor," "Loved One," and "Chief/King." Christian scholar Andrew Walls wrote:

> *"A past is vital for all of us—without it, like the amnesiac man, we cannot know who we are. The prime African theological quest at present is this: what is the past of the African Christian? What is the relationship between Africa's old religions and her new one?"*[57]

To make Christianity serve them instead of having Christianity serve a colonizer's goals, Africans work to view Christianity as an outgrowth or extension of indigenous religions. In a 1993 lecture on African Christianity, Ghanaian theologian Kwame Bediako quoted a "spontaneous adoration of Jesus by an illiterate Ghanaian Christian woman, Christina Afua Gyan, better known as Afua Kuma, a native of the forest town of Obo-Kwahu on the Kwahu mountain ridge in the Eastern Region of Ghana."[58] The piece was published and had consistently sold out. This illiterate woman had captured what African and Western Christian theologians had posited—the reformation of Christianity into an African cultural image. Her poem below reimagines Jesus from a purely West African perspective.

> *Jesus is the grinding stone*
> *on which we sharpen our cutlasses,*
> *before we perform manly deeds.*
> *We have risen at dawn*

to take up our weapons of war,
and join the battle.
Nkrante brafo, You are the Sword Carrier
Okatakyi Birempon: Hero Incomparable
by the time we reach the edge of the battle
the war has already ended.
We turn back, singing praises.

If you go with Jesus to war,
no need for a sword or gun.
The word of his mouth is the weapon
which makes enemies turn and run.

If we walk with Him and we meet with trouble
we are not afraid.
Should the devil himself become a lion
and chase us as his prey,
we shall have no fear Lamb of God!
Satan says he is a wolf
Jesus stretches forth his hand,
and look: Satan is a mouse!
Holy One!

And even in Africa with its black population, another aspect of unmooring Christianity from its colonialist, racist foundations is ridding it of those damned white Jesus images. In 2014, two ministers of Ghana's Methodist Church called for the removal of such images from African Christian worship.

"Rev. Anokye Ababio said the introduction of fake 'White' Jesus images by Europeans is partly to blame for the inferiority complex and dependency syndrome among Africans.

"According to the Superintendent Minister of the Methodist Church Ghana the British used their version of Christianity and the fake 'White' images of Jesus Christ 'as a bedrock or as tool to carry out an agenda which was nefarious and evil in its intent.'

"According to the Superintendent Minister of the Methodist Church Ghana, the European Churches came to Africa on the pretext of a civilising mission but their main agenda was 'to build a European culture of superiority, to dehumanise Africans, and to let Africans see themselves as non-beings.'"[59]

* * *

It is irrational to suggest that Afro-American history has fed us only positive traditions. A people who suffered enslavement and subsequent humiliation and dehumanization for hundreds of years are also bound to accumulate negatives as well. If, embarrassed, we simply pretend that those negatives do not exist, they will continue to fester and do us harm. If, crouched defensively against the inevitable, gleeful attacks some whites launch whenever any of us err, we dare not admit errors, we will continue to suffer from them. Only by confronting the past and acknowledging the positives *and* negatives can we eliminate the latter. And yes, some of those negatives have come down to us in our religious traditions, leading us to think ourselves lesser beings than those who resemble the majority's traditional image of God and his Son. For most of our history, we openly coveted light skin and straight hair. We still do. Today, our pinnacles of beauty remain those who look almost white, from Beyonce to Halle Berry to Alicia Keys. Toni Morrison's 1970 novel, *The Bluest Eye*, tells the story of a black girl who desperately yearns for blond hair and blue eyes. It speaks to colorism, the light-skinned/dark-skinned racism within the Afro-American community and paints portraits of those whose personal value(lessness) has been dictated to them from without. Whoopi Goldberg covered similar ground in her mid 1980s one-woman Broadway show. Worshiping white gods is as great a sickness in an Afro-American man or woman as longing for white skin.

I saw a YouTube video of a man showing black and white passersby pictures of Marcus Garvey, a blond Jesus, and Malcolm X and asking which of these figures was more influential in their lives. The exercise was inelegant and ill-conceived, but what struck me was the black individuals pointing to the white figure of Jesus—not because they chose that figure over Marcus Garvey or Malcolm X, but that they recognized and accepted this blond dude as the Son of God. A blond Jesus should be as foreign to Afro-Americans as a black one is to whites. If forms of Christianity insist on a literal, living Christ born in the region we call the Middle East who walked the earth in human skin, then we must question those forms because a man can walk in only one skin and that skin cannot simultaneously be African, Asian, Caucasian, and everything else. This is America. Race matters. When it no longer does—when the studies and statistics cited in this book no longer apply—then blacks will be free to worship white gods without consequence. Until then, we do so at our peril.

In pointing out the uniquely prodigious spread of Christianity, theologian Andrew Walls wrote:

> *"Each phase of Christian history has seen a transformation of Christianity as it has entered and penetrated another culture. There is no such thing as 'Christian culture' or 'Christian civilization' in the sense that there is an Islamic culture, and an Islamic civilization. There have been several different Christian civilizations already; there may yet be many more. The reason for this lies in the infinite translatability of the Christian faith."*[60]

Afro-Americans have yet to fully remake Christianity in our own image. We have made great strides in that direction, but there are still miles to go. When you consider how fully we have continually transformed various forms of music into jazz or R&B and how we've transformed American dance, or poetry, or sport, our influence on the fundamentals of Christian theological interpretation ran its course in the 1800s. We stopped at liberation theology. (I am ignoring the "prosperity gospel" because it is too gross to dignify.) Liberation was identified as an Afro-American Christian theme quite early. It has since been dressed up in "Black Liberation Theology" robes, but that movement, born in the 1960s and infused with the Black Power ethos, remains "mainly a theology that sees God as concerned with the poor and the weak," in the words of seminal Black Liberation Theology leader Reverend James Cone.

At what point do we stop categorizing ourselves as inherently poor and weak? How do you claim black power when simultaneously insisting on your own poverty and weakness? This was the fatal flaw of the "black power" movement: it was rooted in a presumption of black weakness, if only in its outsized, sometimes parodic reaction to that presumption. Being discriminated against is not synonymous with perpetual suffering. However, that seems to be the conclusion of a black liberation theology dedicated to Afro-American uplift, which states, in the words of religion scholar Anthony Pinn, "God is so intimately connected to the community that suffers, that God becomes a part of that community." If your God loves you more because you suffer, you will suffer; you have normalized suffering. If your God loves you because you are downtrodden, then you have normalized defeat as an acceptable condition of living. Is this much different from the Christianity taught by masters when we were slaves?

Discrimination does not predestine powerlessness or weakness unless you assume that your oppressor will succeed. Is this an assumption that we can self-respect-ingly make in the 21st century? I don't think so. Can Afro-American theological interpretation acknowledge our history, our historical dehumanization and its per-petrators, and the discrimination we continue to fight as well as our liberation without insisting that our status in our God's eyes rests on a debased state?

Afro-American Christianity was built on the assump-tion of our oppression. That is only logical; we birthed it in slavery. However, we are slaves no more. To insist that God loves us because we suffer is beyond retrograde. In religion or in general, power is not the issue. Power ebbs and flows. The issue is Place. Our Place in this American society and in our religiosity is central. A reli-gion of oppression emphasizes the oppressor and makes him central—just as being declared 'white' made one a full citizen. The oppressor's victim is just a by-product. Our Place in our own story must be central. We need to expand the knowledge and practice of an Afro-American theology that sees us as something other than God's favor-ite outcasts. Part of that is convincingly transforming in the Afro-American mind the skin of God's offspring to a deep, deep bronze, thus implying that God-his-father's skin is just as dark as yours and mine.

This can be done. It is being done. We've seen how African biblical interpreters are working to develop readings that make local African culture and traditions central. African Christians have undertaken the multi-generational task of reinterpreting the Bible to suit their own cultural needs. So can we. I acknowledge that strides have been made, but too often—in the vein of Zora Neale Hurston's "Git Back"/"Git Black"—tainted with white centrality and a tinge of self-abnegation.

Has the black church truly and completely freed itself from the prevailing mainstream image of a white God who cursed us and His white Son? Has it determined what steps must be taken to inoculate black youths from this idea to which they're exposed far more regularly than they are to an alternative? Is simply saying "Jesus was black"—based on some vague biblical language—enough when a literal biblical interpretation paints Jesus as a living man and our history and the majority paint that man white? Must our religion of liberation insist that God loves us because we are poor and suffer?

To overcome the negative aspects of the black church legacy, we must critically and fearlessly examine our institutions and traditions and rid them of the remnants of white, racist centrality.

The Methodist/Baptist Christianity from which the black church sprang is not a questioning faith. Its original appeal was its reliance on direct emotion and unquestioning obedience, not critical thinking. However, Christianity has proven an extraordinarily elastic system. In the 21st century, the black church needs to more aggressively codify a theology that puts Afro-Americans in the forefront of our own story, as opposed to presenting us as white folks' collateral damage. It needs to aggressively disseminate a theological system that successfully "metaphorizes" or reconstitutes Jesus such that we see *only* a deity that looks like us—as opposed to one looking like those who tormented us for most of this nation's history. Then we will have freed ourselves from a God that could ever be mistaken for a white man.

EQUAL IS NOT GOOD ENOUGH

"A large part of our self-esteem derives from our group membership," [psychologist Margo] Monteith said. "To the extent we can feel better about our group relative to other groups, we can feel good about ourselves. It's likely a built-in mechanism."[61]

In their much-discussed and often-maligned book, *The Triple Package*, Yale professors Amy Chua and Jeb Rubenfeld, her husband, posited that successful U.S. immigrant cultures had three traits in common. The first, they said, was a sense of superiority. The next was attendant insecurity; the third was "impulse control." The third seems like a rational outgrowth of the first two and an attempt to round out numbers. A book blurb about "the 3 unlikely traits" sounds a lot better than "the 2 unlikely traits."

Those first two struck a chord, as I believe they would with the product of any outsider group striving for better yet fearful that no matter how hard they worked and fought it might prove beyond their reach or, in the case of Afro-Americans, be snatched from their very grasps. Of course, Afro-Americans are not immigrants; our ancestors did not come here voluntarily. Other immigrants were not kidnapped and stripped of every cultural, linguistic, and familial touchstone and held as chattel for generations and within an apartheid subclass for 100 years thereafter. Comparing the circumstances of Afro-Americans to other immigrant groups is treacherous. However, some traits common to outgroups can intersect given sufficient time.

My parents were relentless in their insistence on our family's aspirational exaltation—our status as respectable Negroes (no irony here). Every action we took had to bespeak it and reinforce it. To prove our respectability, we had to be better spoken, better mannered, better groomed—always better and always fearful that we weren't "better" enough. Maintenance of our family's status was a mewling, ravenous baby perpetually at the tit. It would be fed regardless of the pain and the blood.

Chua and Rubenfeld do not discuss Afro-Americans (remember the definition—the American descendants of African slaves) in their book, but they took pains to remove any racial sting by including Nigerians on their list of "winners." However, Afro-American strivers like my parents take the concept of insistent grandiosity conjoined with insecurity and magnify it far beyond the pop psychological cultural asides Chua and Rubenfeld paint. In us, they are grand opera. They are sword and steel. Flesh and blood. They are life and death because the savage insistence on always being better is but a cap on an ever-threatening volcano of imposed self-loathing. It's what keeps psychic devastation at bay when you know that you have gifts, will, ambitions, and dreams equal to those of any man or woman and you know that the world will insist that you dare not—that some would kill you for that insistence.

This is what my parents endured. To do so, I think both had to sacrifice pieces of themselves, as if certain sensitivities or empathies were too big a burden to stand while you battled demons within and without, so they sloughed them off to trudge just a little harder.

In my family, we had the need for superiority and the attendant insecurities and superhuman impulse control that naturally followed, but there was no cultural foundation beneath the aspirational loftiness. Without that, it was just a private snake swallowing its tail.

Growing up, I was familiar with the concept of the "Chosen People." My reading had taught me that early Chinese considered non-Chinese "barbarians" and that rumors of a continued sense of Chinese cultural superiority persist; ditto the Japanese. And of course, the West—England and Germany in particular—ravaged the globe in different ways with their own inflated senses of cultural self.

Knowing of these cultures that crowned themselves superior and revisiting the Margo Monteith quote cited at the top of this chapter and elsewhere in this book, I searched for instances in which Afro-Americans crowned ourselves generally culturally superior. I could not find any. Yes, there are many spheres we dominate, but do we instill the idea in young people that they come from a stock that is more courageous, more resolute, and more resourceful than any other American people have had to be? Do we credit ourselves with our mercy and restraint (good or bad)? We certainly know that if anyone had done to white Americans what they have done to us, it would have been cause for nothing less than a genocidal rampage against the perpetrators. Do we credit ourselves with being a sufficiently formidable force that in 2011 most Americans assumed we represented 20% of the population instead of the 12% we comprised at the time?[62] There is nary an aspect of this country's governance that our presence has not inordinately influenced—from the structure of our governmental institutions to the rights and freedoms we profess to love. Do we credit ourselves as the people who forced this nation to recognize that it failed to practice what it preached regarding equality under the law or with forcing this nation to legally enforce the concepts it claimed to hold dear but had instead betrayed? Do we place ourselves front and center in America's story?

Equality is a demotion. I do not feel we are equal to the majority of men and women with whom we share this land. I feel that we are superior. We have had to be. They have not clawed their way out of 188 years of various forms of legally and socially enforced bondage and subjugation to compel the offending nation to change its laws and habits. They have not, despite 188 years of violence and non- and second-class citizenship, colored every aspect of this culture from music to dance to speech to literature. We have come further. We have overcome more. We have achieved breathtaking things.

Instead, we have settled for seeking to be equal—not only in the eyes of the law, but in our own. It's as if our traumatic American experience has robbed us of the capability to see ourselves aggrandized in ways endemic to other cultures. However, it's because of that trauma that it's more imperative that we correct this cultural diffidence. When you have a nation still projecting its bias in media, housing, employment, and law enforcement, you must counter with something stronger than the weak tea of "equality." We need pedestals on which to stand. If we're to have darts hurled at us, the least we can do is look down on the ones doing the throwing.

How do we do that? We do it through cultural self-education. It is done through a course of learning spread over the formative years of young Afro-American lifetimes that teach us honestly where we came from, what formed us, the myriad directions in which we've traveled, and who we have come to be.

HISTORICAL AND CULTURAL
EDUCATION ON THE JEWISH MODEL

I am proposing nothing less than an extracurricular course of study for Afro-American children and any African-Americans or others who identify with us designed to teach our young who we are and the horrors, triumphs, and in-betweens that tell the story of how we came to invent ourselves in this America. As young Jews learn about their culture and history in Hebrew schools, Afro-American children should learn about their culture and history through Afro-American curricula. Imagine black 6-year-olds learning about 18th-century West Africa— its landscape, customs, arts, and traditions, outside of a white Western frame. In such a context, this ancestry can become a source of fascination, as opposed to the retrograde embarrassment as it's often portrayed through Western lenses.

Imagine black 8-year-olds learning how African traders kidnapped their forebears and delivered them to white slave traders on the African coast. They'd learn the savagery of the Middle Passage and that, despite slavers' brutal efforts to quash resistance, at least 10% of slave ships experienced some form of insurrection. The actual number of slave ship insurrections is probably substantially higher; if a rebellion were successful and the ship's crew killed, the ship would simply be labeled "lost."

Young Afro-American students would learn about the world the slaves made in this new land, the daily waltzes of accommodation and rebellion they danced with slave masters, the passive and active resistance in which they participated.

They would learn about the founding of this slavery-bound America from an Afro-American point of view. Imagine learning early in our young lives how the American promise of freedom and justice came not to apply to us, and how all the power of the State was focused on denying not only our rights but our humanity. We'd simultaneously learn how, from the first, we sourced our humanity to evolve a homegrown culture that would grow over centuries into the tour de force it is today; how, from the first, we fought for recognition of our rights to the American promise.

As these students grew older, they'd learn to be simultaneously repulsed by the self-serving hypocrisy of the Constitution's authors, even as they admired the estimable sentiments they had the vision to articulate, but neither the character nor the integrity to fulfill. To learn American history from our own point of view is to see this nation burst from the womb committing original sins that it would spend the rest of its history grappling with. Eighty-five years after this country's founding, through a document that coyly never mentions slavery but enshrines it into the nation's DNA, the country would fight a civil war in which hundreds of thousands would die. To this day, 150 years later, the nation is still psychologically riven along those original north/south battle lines. In a *New York Times* piece on the anniversary of the surrender of confederate forces at Appomattox, history professor Gregory Downs wrote, "Years after the 1865 surrender, the novelist and veteran Albion Tourgée said that the South 'surrendered at Appomattox, and the North has been surrendering ever since.'"

Honing young reading skills on Zora Neale Hurston's collection of black folk tales would provide cultural context for the historical lessons students learn. Books akin to Lesa Cline-Ransome's *Light in the Darkness: A Story About How Slaves Learned in Secret*, which tells the tale of how a young slave risked her life to learn to read, would teach the many forms rebellion can take.

As they grew older, students would learn to accurately track this nation's history and our places in it—slave labor's seminal contribution to the growth and wealth of this nation—a value never acknowledged and a debt never paid. The book *Jubilee: The Emergence of African-American Culture* from the Schomburg Center for Research in Black Culture provides a succinct catalog of slave labor's prominence in the United States economy.

"Each plantation economy was part of a larger national and international political economy. The cotton plantation economy, for instance, is generally seen as part of the regional economy of the American South. By the 1830s, "cotton was king" indeed in the South. It was also king in the United States, which was competing for economic leadership in the global political economy. Plantation-grown cotton was the foundation of the antebellum southern economy. . . .

But the American financial and shipping industries were also dependent on slave-produced cotton. So was the British textile industry. Cotton was not shipped directly to Europe from the South. Rather, it was shipped to New York and then transshipped to England and other centers of cotton manufacturing in the United States and Europe.

As the cotton plantation economy expanded throughout the southern region, banks and financial houses in New York supplied the loan capital and/or investment capital to purchase land and slaves.[63]

Students would learn about the promise and betrayals of reconstruction—how Afro-American former slaves educated themselves, won elected offices, how some founded businesses and banks until the United States allowed the terrorists of Jim Crow to destroy all the progress we had made. They'd learn about those former slaves who, having known nothing but literal and figurative chains their entire lives, were left unprepared to live much differently without them.

They'd learn about black outlaws and lawmen in the Old West, black freedmen in the Indian Territories, the Great Migrations of the early 20th century that transformed national politics and culture, and the urbanization of the black community as we fled Jim Crow in search of opportunity in the north. They would learn how racist zoning and exclusionary/predatory lending robbed Afro-Americans of an equal chance at building wealth all over this nation.

Within this course of study, students would learn who they are and where they come from—and they would learn it from us.

The Education/Integration/Self-Education Conundrum

In a May 2014 article in *The Atlantic*, titled "Segregation Now . . . ," writer Nikole Hannah-Jones looked at the resegregation of the schools in Tuscaloosa, Alabama. In the late 1970s, court orders had mandated school integration, which was achieved through merging the formerly black and white high schools into a single, integrated entity. The school prospered.

However, in the 2000s, hundreds of school districts were released from court orders, allowing them to resegregate. Or rather, the courts allowed whites to remove themselves from the unwelcome presence of blacks.

"But since 2000, judges have released hundreds of school districts, from Mississippi to Virginia, from court-enforced integration, and many of these districts have followed the same path as Tuscaloosa's—back toward segregation. Black children across the South now attend majority-black schools at levels not seen in four decades. Nationally, the achievement gap between black and white students, which greatly narrowed during the era in which schools grew more integrated, widened as they became less so."[64]

I have discussed why I think integration is critical. Afro-American students need to be in proximity to whites to literally demystify them. At the same time, it's imperative to simultaneously teach even very young Afro-American children how we stand apart from the historical majority. Integration should march hand in hand with self-taught cultural distinction.

Sometimes, however, that's just not possible. The high school in the article resegregated for the sole reason that white parents did not want their children attending school with blacks. This was a high-achieving school, without racial discord in its corridors.

"Central was not just a renowned local high school. It was one of the South's signature integration success stories. . . . Within a few years, Central emerged as a powerhouse that snatched up National Merit Scholarships and math-competition victories just as readily as it won trophies in football, track, golf."[65]

Three smaller schools have replaced the once integrated powerhouse. Central High School now serves the poorest residents, 99% of whom are black. Nearby white neighborhoods have been gerrymandered into overwhelmingly white school districts. Again, there was nothing wrong with the integrated school. It educated its students very well. The only thing wrong with it was that it forced white children to see and interact with black ones. Such resegregation is happening all over the South as districts are released from court-ordered desegregation under the assumption that school districts and parents can be trusted to keep base hatreds at bay. That assumption is wrong:

> "According to an analysis by ProPublica, the number of apartheid schools nationwide has mushroomed from 2,762 in 1988—the peak of school integration—to 6,727 in 2011."[66]

Integration would be ideal, but it will often be impossible. Nevertheless, self-education in our history and culture—on its own—can go a long way toward demystifying the majority in young Afro-Americans' eyes and providing the tools they need to counter the various forms of prejudice they will likely encounter in America.

They will learn that whites too often seek segregation because one way or another, we will always stand apart and as a challenge to their conception of self. Of course, we stand apart visually; our skin is usually darker, our hair nappier, our features broader. In addition, our history is grotesquely and spectacularly unique. Because of these factors, we will never "blend into" America. Our difference—and our history—is drawn all over our faces and bodies. A bloody history is etched on our skin, and it's a history that at the very least discomfits a good proportion of whites in this country. Our skin is not like fog; it does not burn off over time. It is *always* there—chattering, whispering about our history—and America's crimes—whether we or anyone else likes it.

White conservatives and their black abettors insist that if we would only think sufficiently white-ly—gleefully view America and the world through a White Racial Frame, accepting the myths and illusions that deny our history—white folks would stop seeing our skin and all it represents and treat us with the respect due "honorary whites." But they're wrong because so many will always, at some level, fear history's chattering. They fear that the crimes they committed will rise from the background and roar, deafening, and they will have the unenviable choice of cowering in horror at that grisly sound and what it screams about their past or trying to outshout it with epithets insisting that we deserved it then and deserve it still.

We will always stand apart. Our choice is whether we stand on a pedestal or in a ditch. The ditch is wide and deep; it was dug for us a long time ago, and we were thrown into it. The pedestal we have yet to build. This is not about power. It is about ownership. It is about owning our past and the culture that it bore. It is about viewing this country and our countrymen through the lens that past and culture bequeath us. Through that lens, they will look . . . *less* than they do through the goggles they strapped on us so long ago. They will not like being less; well, neither have we. Tough shit.

Why must we learn our history and culture from a young age at the feet of other Afro-Americans? While writing this, I read a report of former New York Mayor Rudy Giuliani telling a conservative audience that Obama doesn't "love America" and wasn't "brought up" to love the country in the same way as the former mayor and his conservative audience.

To view America through the same eyes as Rudy Giuliani's would mean gouging out our own. Rudy Giuliani's ancestors were not chained and dragged to this country, robbed of homes, cultures, religions, families, and every belonging and sold into slavery for life. His forebears were not legally denied access to homes, jobs, educations, medical care, food, and the vote until about 50 years ago. No, I do not see America the way he does, nor "love" America the way he does because America spent most of its history savaging me and mine. I don't even know what a man like Giuliani means by "love" America. He clearly has no love for Afro-Americans. Does he hold Jews and Latinos in equal contempt? How much must he diminish America to profess such undying love? What critical parts of her must he amputate such that he can make love to her mutilated corpse? I can acknowledge this country's great aspirations and achievements while remembering the humiliations it heaped upon those like me. Whites would do no less were they in our shoes. This country wields the death penalty—a punishment of vengeance, not justice or prevention. Americans hold a grudge. We believe in revenge, yet when it comes to Afro-Americans, whites get suddenly Christian, insisting that we shout our forgetfulness and forgiveness to prove we sufficiently "love" America. I think we're asked to testify to our love because the majority are well aware of the reasons we have to hate, and more importantly, unlike us, faced with similar circumstances, so many of them would have fully succumbed to vengeful, violent hatred long ago.

I do not know what white men like Giuliani mean when they say they "love" America, for the America they profess to love so often ignores or diminishes me. What does it mean to love a country in which, according to a 2012 Associated Press poll, 51% of Americans expressed explicit antiblack bias?[67] Even if you believe that number to be wildly exaggerated, reduce it to 30%. Does that make it all better? That would mean that 30% of the population is still willing to see me less protected by the law than they, more deserving to rot in prison or to die unjustly from the bullet of a cop's gun. That means that there are citizens of this country with whom I share practically nothing—not a sense of justice, nor right and wrong, nor the meaning of the Constitution or the Bill of Rights. In fact, there are citizens whose attitudes are beyond anathema to me in that they would make it legal once more to deny me those things that my forebears shed blood to see that I had equal access to. So no, I do not pretend to blindly "love" America. I am Afro-American. I don't need to prove anything by mewling about how much I love it. My father fought for this country as it spat on him as a man. Countless others like him fought and died for it despite every institution in the country insistently denying their humanity. I AM America—in all of its ideals and hypocrisies, its bloodiness and lies, its promise and its betrayals. I embody every last one. I have nothing to prove. No Afro-American man or woman does.

See Through Black Eyes

By Leonce Gaiter
Newsweek, December 9, 2014

We know that when Darren Wilson and many of his defenders see a black man, they see someone who "looks like a demon," and someone who has the extra/sub-human ability to "bulk up to run through" bullets.

We know this image of black men from an entire history of racist stereotypes. The image that Darren Wilson successfully invoked before the Missouri grand jury was the same image of monstrous black bucks lusting for white blood that propelled D.W. Griffith's 1915 racist masterwork, *Birth of a Nation*.

Throughout American history, most images of blacks have been created and presented by whites—and throughout the overwhelming majority of this nation's history, the nation and its people have been institutionally racist. Only for the past 50 years have blacks enjoyed laws aimed at granting us equal treatment under the law. For the previous 188, we lived as slaves and a sub-species of citizen.

However, throughout that history, blacks have developed our own images of whites, images buttressed not by the toxic stew of fear, hatred, and guilt that boils in white America's kitchen, but by history and lived experience.

Imagine that my southern-born parents taught me that each white man or woman I encountered was a potential enemy, that each should be seen as someone who might deny me a job for which I was qualified, might deny me schooling, housing, freedom—even deny me my life.

Imagine they told me that whites often saw me through the twisted lens of a self-serving lie—the lie of my otherness, my laziness, my ignorance, of my propensity to violence—lies they told themselves to justify their vicious brutality, and their tolerance of it. Imagine I was told that to forget that in the face of the evidence would make me the basest kind of fool, deserving of whatever harm befell me at vicious white men's hands.

Imagine that my striving, southern-born parents taught me that seeking equality with whites would be a demotion. A people who tolerated for centuries the enslavement of others, who enshrined chattel butchery in their founding documents, and then, most importantly, denied the existence of blood when their hands dripped with the stuff—these were not people with whom you sought parity. These were negative object lessons to whose depths you swore never to fall.

Imagine that my righteously angry southern-born parents taught me that the American Dream was for whites, that American justice was for white people, that Disney-esque happy endings were for white people.

Now, imagine that we're not imagining. This is what my parents taught me—that every white man or woman was a creature that I should approach as I would a strange, stray dog, just as likely to bite your hand off as wag its tail. They taught me and my siblings to be wary at every encounter, and constantly steel ourselves against what ill will might erupt from white skin.

It worked. Like any good parents, ours prepared us for the world as it is, and by any standards, we are a highly accomplished set of children. I credit much of that to the hard lessons our parents taught us.

Now, imagine once more—this time that I, and those like me represent the majority, the state and its power, and that we have guns on our hips, badges on our chests, and the power to shoot you without consequence.[68]

The Difference between "Black History" and "American History from an Afro-American Perspective"

When I speak of teaching American history from our perspective, many will immediately insist that we do so already through Black History Month curricula and through African-American Studies departments in many colleges.

Again, I want to make clear that I am not discussing college-level instruction. I am talking about teaching the young. It is also important to note the difference between what most call teaching black history and what I'm suggesting.

Black history instruction as I've been exposed to it treats us as Rosencrantz and Guildenstern to America's Hamlet. We walk onto America's stage and provide some informational plot grease and then disappear for very long stretches as the principals continue their more central business.

I'm suggesting that we cast ourselves as the main characters and rewrite the action from our own point of view.

In most classrooms, we are a sidebar to American history. I'm suggesting that we become the central text. As discussed, America's founding looks very different when shown through an Afro-American lens. For instance, black men and women did not write the Constitution or personally influence its drafting. However, our presence was central to the document becoming what it was and creating the nation America would become. The Three-Fifths Compromise provided slave-holding states with additional national representation based on the number of men and women they enslaved, an act that taints American institutions to this day. In further deference to Southern slave states, the Constitution made it impossible to ban the slave trade until the year 1800. This further enshrined within the new nation's society, foundational culture, and laws the degenerate institution of slavery.

No, this is not the same thing children would learn in any decent history class. For instance, California's guide to fifth grade Common Core standards describes what students will learn about the framing of the U.S. Constitution.

"With an understanding of the framers in mind, students can participate in mock Constitutional conventions to consider the document's major compromises. In the Great Compromise, the framers divided the federal government's legislative power between two houses, one which

represented all states equally and another in which state population accounted for state representatives. The framers also agreed with the 3/5 compromise, that three-fifths of the slave population would be counted in determining states' representation in the national legislature and for imposing property taxes. Lastly, the Northwest Ordinance codified the process for admitting new states. "[69]

For us, the Three-Fifths Compromise is not the equivalent of the process for admitting new states. It is the beginning of our American journey; it is a betrayal, at the moment of its birth, of this country's promise. To us, it is nothing like the technical mechanism for admitting new states. It gave slave states over one-third more electoral votes and congressional seats than they would otherwise have had, weighted the electoral scales in favor of those states, opened the door to new slave states, and impacted Thomas Jefferson's election as president.

In a foreword to his book *Negro President: Jefferson and the Slave Power,* historian Gary Wills describes what he calls a "fault line" dividing historians in America. "The division," he wrote, "is between those who think that slavery is central to [American] history and those who think it is peripheral."

If we accede to the legitimacy of such a "debate," we accept the insignificance of our place in American history and so the legitimacy of our treatment in America. If it is *not* central to America's history that ideals of freedom and democracy were befouled by the acceptance of slavery, then our living and suffering under and beyond that institution are insignificant. If that is the case, our histories are insignificant. I do not accept that. It is a lie. No Afro-American child should be exposed to such a dehumanizing idea without the tools to damn it as the lie that it is.

Learning American history from an Afro-American perspective is to question every generally accepted precept about the founding of this nation. The framers of the Constitution feared that Southern states would shun the union unless slavery was not only allowed but allowed to tip the balance of power in favor of its practice and preservation. The framers of the Constitution acquiesced, trading our bodies for their Union.

Similarly, Abraham Lincoln was willing to sacrifice our lives and liberty to the cause of preserving the United States. In his letter to editor Horace Greeley, Lincoln wrote:

> *"If I could save the Union without freeing any slave I would do it, and if I could save it by freeing all the slaves I would do it; and if I could save it by freeing some and leaving others alone I would also do that. What I do about slavery, and the colored race, I do because I believe it helps to save the Union; and what I forbear, I forbear because I do not believe it would help to save the Union."*

And he was not alone:

> *"It was as Frederick Douglass said in Boston in 1865, that the Civil War was begun 'in the interests of slavery on both sides. The South was fighting to take slavery out of the Union, and the North fighting to keep it in the Union; the South fighting to get it beyond the limits of the United States Constitution, and the North fighting for the old guarantees;—both despising the Negro, both insulting the Negro.'"*[70]

Again, our lives and bodies were the price Lincoln and most of America were willing to pay for the preservation of the United States. Now ask yourselves, whose bodies would you sacrifice for this nation? Whom would you enslave to keep her? To preserve the United States, would you satisfy the desires of powerful men to rape women at will? To preserve the United States, would you satisfy a majority desire to reduce people to unpaid servitude, relegate them to labor camps, or treat them as commodities that some could buy and sell like dogs? What moral outrage would be so great that you would say to yourself that the cost is not worth paying—that doing so would tear the very soul from the country that you claim to shield?

We must learn that some Americans' very concept of freedom is basted in this nation's founding in slavery; in particular, the slaveholding South's concept of the sanctity of personal property—in the form of black bodies— as the essence of liberty. To them liberty was not defined as freedom from fear, ignorance, or want—but freedom to dispose of what you own—the people you own—in any manner you saw fit regardless of the damage done. This definition festers in the conservative mindset to this day. There is a reason that America ranks poorly and sometimes last among wealthy nations in measures like infant mortality, health care availability, family leave, and childcare.

> "The U.S. rate of 6.1 infant deaths per 1,000 live births masks considerable state-level variation. If Alabama were a country, its rate of 8.7 infant deaths per 1,000 would place it slightly behind Lebanon in the world rankings. Mississippi, with its 9.6 deaths, would be somewhere between Botswana and Bahrain."[71]

It is an affront to some Americans' old South conception of "liberty" to be forced to participate economically in the community even as they benefit from being part of it. They don't want to pay for the dreaded "other's" health care because their tax money should not be used to subsidize anything for anyone they disfavor. If the community includes those they revile, they reject the concept of community. They feel about their money the way Southern planters felt about their slaves. To antebellum Southerners, "Nothing was more essential to liberal freedom than the right of self-government and protection of property against interference by the state."[72] Again, freedom from want and ignorance is not their definition of liberty but rather freedom from government constraints on the use, misuse, or disposition of personal property.

Significant traditional American concepts of "liberty" and the sanctity of property were midwifed on the slave plantation, and all Americans, black and white, are paying for it. The South "surrendered at Appomattox, and the North has been surrendering ever since."

To learn our history from our own point of view is to grapple with these outcomes of our presence in this land. It is to do what the majority would never allow in mainstream institutions—question the morality of this nation's founding. We must, because failure to do so is to reinforce the idea that we exist to be sacrificed to her. Failure to question means that America had the right to forfeit us, our rights, our very selves. Failure to question is to enforce the idea that our lives are valueless, that we remain commodities, a bloody kind of coal to be incinerated when this country needs fuel.

Most of the nations on this earth were born in the basest sort of sin. Wars, butchery, murder, theft, genocide—they all played roles in drawing the maps by which we humans define ourselves. America is not unique in the ignoble aspects of her origin. But Afro-Americans, along with Native Americans, are unique in that it was on our backs and corpses on which America claimed to build a shining city on the hill while ignoring the gore at her feet. And of course, it is utterly disingenuous to claim that we cannot judge white America's ancestors by today's standards. Thomas Jefferson simultaneously paid homage to liberty while calling the institution of slavery in which he freely participated "a system 'one hour of which is fraught with more misery, than ages of that which [the colonists] rose in rebellion to oppose.'"[73]

To study this is to accept the conundrum that we are quintessentially and irrevocably *of* this nation that despised and debased us—so much so that we fought in her wars when we were largely barred from gaining work and reward according to our gifts, living where we wished, owning what we could afford, accessing financial resources, adequately educating our children, freely exercising our right to vote, or getting a fair hearing before the law. To study is to realize the magic we conjured in wresting a primary place in the cultural and civic life of this nation that treated us so viciously and, in some ways, continues to do so.

To study America from an Afro-American perspective is to acknowledge the extraordinary individuals who managed firsts—the Jackie Robinsons, the Madame C.J. Walkers—while realizing that the bulk of our progress was not due to such unique combinations of pluck, tenacity, talent, and luck but due instead to the more mundane, daily labors of seamstresses, porters, janitors, lawyers, maids, soldiers, preachers, doctors, and all the other black men and women who, one by one and time after time, and sometimes in the most unassuming ways, demanded what was due them and paved the way for something more for those who came after.

Imagine the benefits of empowering parents with a curriculum that guided their children toward an Afro-American–centric take on this country's history and our place in it. Imagine if these lessons were bolstered by in-class sessions that reinforced and expanded on the lessons learned in the home (perhaps in black churches, should they choose to retake a central place in secular Afro-American culture). Imagine black youth who learned their history from us instead of those who've spent a history oppressing us.

To see people like yourself violated in every way throughout a nation's history—it is repugnant. Aspects of the history we must teach our children will provoke rage. The mainstream (too often with our willing consent) has worked to deny us that inevitable, fundamental human response. "You must not be angry," we're told, "for then you'll be reviled as the 'angry black' man or woman." What becomes of rage subsumed? It turns inward. We must teach each other that rage is part of learning your history in America. And we must teach each other what to do with that rage—how to transform it into drive, knowledge, accomplishment, and a clear-eyed view of the country and world in which we live.

I've heard folks ask pleadingly, "Where are our happy endings? Where are our fairy tales?" as if someone should be advocating feel-good lessons full of invincible black warriors who ceaselessly triumph over white evils—as if someone should propose a set of continual black superhero lessons. I don't know how to respond to that. Frankly, I am a little appalled by the question. First, the assumption that anyone is due a fairy-tale ending is grotesque to me and stands in contravention of the unbroken rules of life on earth as I know it. It's also a symptom of a uniquely American disease (but that's another discussion altogether). However, to suggest that the truth of our history is not good enough—that the mass of the men and women who came before us are somehow insufficiently inspiring or worthy of study— that appalls me. It means that we have bought the lie of our unworthiness. It means we believe that the ordinary struggles that, over time, achieved extraordinary results were insignificant.

There is no shame whatsoever in our past—not in our subtle nor overt fights against our enslavement, not in our acts of self-preservation, and certainly not in the culture we molded from our abused state. If any Afro-American man, woman, or child fears looking backward out of shame, he or she is defeated already.

There are whole histories out there, the details of which are outrageously empowering and about which most of us know so little. They are stories worth telling ourselves. For example, in his book *The Story of American Freedom*, historian Eric Foner wrote:

> *"The [American] revolution inspired widespread hopes that slavery could be removed from American life. Most dramatically, slaves themselves appreciated that by defining freedom as a universal right, the revolutionists had*

*devised a rhetoric that could be deployed against chattel
bondage. The language of liberty echoed in slave com-
munities, North and South. Living amid freedom but
denied its substance, slaves appropriated the patriotic
ideology for their own purposes. The first concrete steps
toward emancipation were 'Freedom petitions'—argu-
ments for manumission presented to New England's
courts and legislatures in the early 1770s by enslaved
African-Americans. Once the War for Independence
began, the British offered freedom to slaves who joined
the royal cause. Nearly one hundred thousand, including one-quarter of all the slaves in South Carolina,
deserted their owners (although not a few were subsequently reenslaved in the West Indies)."*[74]

Years ago, I happened upon a 19th-century photo of five
Native American and Afro-American teens. The caption
said that in 1895, this group, the Rufus Buck Gang, went
on a violent 13-day rampage through Indian Territory in
a vain attempt to wrest it back from whites. The photo fascinated me. The five stood abreast, shackled, and looking
remarkably young. The leader, Rufus Buck, was half-black
and half-Indian, another was African-American, and the
others Creek Indian. The photo had that grim, grainy
urgency so typical of early photography, with blank,
unsmiling faces and an air of deathly stillness. The caption informed that they had stood trial in the courtroom
of the notorious "Hanging Judge," Isaac Parker, and had
been executed for their crimes.

This story of black and Indian teenagers fighting against injustice with equal injustice—through a vengeance-obsessed murder spree—fascinated me partially because it was so unlike any piece of American history I had been taught. I also wanted to know what kind of America it was in which blacks and Indians mixed so freely and so familiarly with whites that they had the sovereignty to terrorize them. Research led me to a world I hadn't known existed: an Indian Territory that, at the turn of the century, housed more whites than Indians as well as a township of black freedmen founded by some who had fled west. Blacks, Indians, and whites all lived with a surprising degree of integration in the "Indian Territory" that we now call Oklahoma. Judge Parker's principal deputy was a black man named Bass Reeves. Famed outlaw Cherokee Bill was half black, raised by his black grandmother. Creek Lighthorse law enforcement worked with the U.S. Marshals to track down the Buck Gang.

I learned all I could about the Rufus Buck Gang and the time and place they lived in. They were vicious and childish and used every foul means at their disposal to achieve their ends. In other words, they acted just like the white American historical actors we hear so much about—those who stole and murdered (Jesse James, Bonnie and Clyde) and limited themselves to murder (John Wesley Hardin) and rape (Thomas Jefferson [Sally Hemmings was a 14-year-old slave when he began bedding her]). Vicious, yet seemingly childlike, the Buck

Gang took every lesson to be learned from blacks' and Indians' treatment at the hands of whites and fed them back in kind—to the horror of all Indian Territory residents—black, red, and white. Both their violence and self-righteousness were prototypically American. I based a book on them because they presented a fascinating bridge between races and eras and their rampage and subsequent execution heralded the end of the Old West as much as any other violent American set piece. The stories of our madmen and miscreants can tell us just as much and sometimes more than tales of our saints. Tales of revenge are just as valid and crucial as those of forgiveness and reconciliation.

But these are stories you will never hear in mainstream classrooms. You will probably not see such stories made into movies or TV shows or on the best-seller lists. As noted earlier, these stories do not conform to the image white America likes to see of us—passive and victimized. Yes, we have been victimized throughout our history, but rarely passive. From men and women risking all to overtake slave ships or throwing themselves from them rather than live in chains, fleeing owners to fight with the British against the nascent nation of slave owners, to doing our damnedest to turn a religion introduced to keep us enslaved into a fire for our liberation, we have actively fought. Sometimes we fought foolishly, but who hasn't? The stories of those fights—be they righteous, rageful, or otherwise—they are part of our history. America should no longer be allowed to deny them to us.

A Private Conversation

From Marcus Garvey to Malcolm X, black leaders have insisted that we "do for ourselves." This has principally been presented and interpreted as an all-or-nothing-at-all proposition—a zero-sum game requiring either mass migration or self-segregation. It requires neither. It requires that we finally shed the empty, color-based political designation foisted upon us and acknowledge our American historical and cultural distinction instead and organize it into courses of study appropriate to our children. It's probably imperative to do this outside the purview of mainstream institutions. White hands cannot rule this joystick. Most white institutions would have no business funding it. Government affiliation or accountability should be nil for the reasons noted clearly above: large swaths of the majority haven't the courage, self-confidence, or stomach for these truths.

This must be frank talk among ourselves, without concern for how the majority view what's said. As we teach the young about the distinctive viciousness of American chattel slavery and how it put to shame the horrors of many other forms of slavery throughout history, we will be accused of teaching children to hate. No such thing will occur. We will teach children the facts. If some feel that those facts lead inevitably to hate, then it's both a cultural mirror and this nation's historical actions that they need to review.

This is what we must "do for ourselves." Separating ourselves from and denying ourselves this country's fruits is cutting off our noses to spite our faces; it's acquiescence to the superiority the majority attempted to don by calling themselves 'white.' This country's fruits are ours; we did much of the planting and harvesting. We've shed as much blood for this land as any other people in it. The American descendants of African slaves are a cultural entity born principally of this America—like it or not. What I am suggesting is simply a defanging of the dual consciousness W.E.B. DuBois described over 100 years ago. I suggest that Afro-Americans teach each other who we are and where we came from instead of letting the majority do it from frameworks too often historically racist or defensive in their willful ignorance and distortion of the facts of this nation's history.

I believe that this is our next crucial step. It is nothing novel. It's not sexy like marching down streets. It's not likely to attract the mainstream cameras of the six o'clock news. However, it can provide future generations with the tools they need to counter the prevailing biases, preconceptions, and lies about who we are and our place in this country that litter American institutions. It can relieve us of the shame of believing that we were passive recipients of the filth the majority directed toward us.

With a powerful counternarrative running throughout their formative years, Afro-American children and young adults will be equipped to accept the mainstream as their own instead of fearing and deriding it as 'white.' Perhaps then they will be better able to demand their rightful places within it. But with Afro-American self-education, they will also have a firm grasp of their special, separate gift, which is the culture and history of Afro-America—an American history that stands separate and apart from that which many in the majority want us to know. They will be able to identify the lies and omissions that occur in their mainstream classrooms, and regardless of whether their teachers or classmates accept their corrections, they will have the facts they need to see their teachers and classmates as lacking—not themselves.

Every black youth should know that this country and its culture owe a great deal to us even as it denies our cultural value and pretends that our contributions are marginal at best, and negative at worst.

"Black nationalists have always perceived something unmentionable about America that integrationists dare not acknowledge—that white supremacy is not merely the work of hotheaded demagogues, or a matter of false consciousness, but a force so fundamental to America that it is difficult to imagine the country without it."[75]

We should not have to imagine such a country without the stain of white supremacy. We should teach it. We should redraw this country within our own racial frame and present that to young Afro-Americans so they can grow their pride and sense of place from it.

The same majority that oversaw and tolerated the crimes against us for 188 years are now the ones who look at us after 50 years of "equality" that often exists on paper only and tsk that we should be "over it." Some insist that they have "made up" for slavery, ignoring the subsequent 100+ years of American apartheid, ignoring the sickening stream of facts and figures that clearly indict many significant portions of our national apparatus (e.g., education and justice systems) as systemically deformed by our history of race hatred. They point to the 12 years of Reconstruction, which were severed abruptly and replaced with apartheid Jim Crow laws and Klan terrorism that did their damnedest to put us back in chains. They point to a few years of affirmative action as if they acted as antidote to the centuries of affirmative action for whites that denied us access to this country's bounty regardless of our talents or gifts.

Ours is a history that a significant portion of America actively wants to forget, a forgetfulness to which many of the rest are happy to acquiesce. A healthy chunk of fellow citizens want to behave and legislate as if our history— which is partly a history of their own self-debasement— never happened. We cannot let them. Do they insist that Southerners forgo their treasured Civil War illusions? Do they insist that Jews "get over it" and stop talking about their European oppression or the Holocaust? No. In fact, the majority cheer the ideal of "never forget." Do they insist that we forget World War II or the Revolutionary War? No. They only insist that we forget *our* history.

Speaking from Mozambique Island off the African coast, where Africans were herded onto ships for lifetimes of slavery, Lonnie Bunch, founding director of the Smithsonian National Museum of African American History and Culture, was asked what a black man saw at such a place. He said:

> *"[A] combination of unbelievable pain, a sense of anger, a sense of loss, but also an amazing sense of optimism."*
>
> *"I want people to realize how amazingly strong the enslaved people must have been to survive that voyage and to survive, in essence, their time on the cross," Bunch says.*
>
> *"I wish I could, as part of my gift to America, give African Americans that sense of pride in a part of their history that many shy away from."*

Finding the strength to endure slavery is a great achievement but, for us, a lesser one. From that history, we found the tools to break our chains. An unprejudiced view of our history from our own point of view is vital because, from it, we built a culture that transformed a nation.

The majority will not remember our history for us. In fact, the 2016 election has proven that a significant portion of the population has, at the very least, a massive tolerance for bigotry and race hatred as well as a soft spot for the American foundational concept of white supremacy. This group has no lofty dreams of brotherhood that include us. The majority of the group who identify as white will not fight for our equal rights. In fact, they will often rationalize and even cheer the prospect of injustice aimed at us. The majority will not teach us what came before such that we can celebrate its legacy. That majority will not build the foundation we need to see past the warped mirror they themselves have held up to us. They will not build the foundation we need to elevate ourselves as the indelible cultural force that we've become.

Color-based, culture-free identities were foisted on us hundreds of years ago. Those identities bred "nigger" and "colored" and they cannot do this work. Only Afro-Americans can—people not shackled by white supremacist concepts of color-based race, but elevated by a vital, ineradicable, often nightmarish shared history—and ennobled by the indelible culture we've fashioned from it.

References

1. Shankar Vedantam, "Psychiatry Ponders Whether Extreme Bias Can Be an Illness," Washington Post, December 10, 2005.

2. M.T. Wang and J. P. Huguley, "Parental Racial Socialization as a Moderator of the Effects of Racial Discrimination on Educational Success Among African American Adolescents," *Child Development*, 83(5), June 2012, pp. 1716–1731.

3. Roger Highfield, "DNA Survey Finds All Humans Are 99.9pc the Same," *The Telegraph*, December 20, 2002.

4. Theodore Allen, "Summary of the Argument of *The Invention of the White Race*," (VI, par. 35) 1998.

5. Ibid.

6. Ibid., VI, par. 47.

7. W.E.B. Du Bois, *Black Reconstruction*, 1935.

8. "Albert Murray's Omni-America," August 26, 2013, Harvard University Press blog.

9. Omri Ben-Shahar, "The Non-Voters Who Decided the Election: Trump Won Because of Lower Democratic Turnout," *Forbes*, November 17, 2016.

10. John Blake, "Why I'm Tired of Hearing About 'That' Civil Rights Movement," *CNN*, August 25, 2014.

11. Jacoba Urist, "Who Should Decide How Students Learn About America's Past?" *The Atlantic*, February 24, 2015.

12. Ronald Reagan, Radio Address to the Nation on Civil Rights.

13. Paul Rockwell, "Giving False Testimony on King's Views," *Los Angeles Times*, January 17, 1997.

14. Alyssa Figueroa, "MLK's Most Famous, Least Understood 'I Have a Dream' Speech," *AlterNet*, August 21, 2013.

15. "Teaching the Movement: The State of Civil Rights Education in the United States 2011, a report by the Southern Poverty Law Center's Teaching Tolerance Program," September 2011.

16. Cecil Brown, "Richard Wright's Complexes and Black Writing Today," *Speech and Power*, Volume 1, Gerald Early, ed.

17. Margery Otto and Herbert Perkins, "A Reading of Feagin's *The White Racial Frame: Centuries of Racial Framing and Counter-Framing*," January 2011.

18. Ibid.

19. "A New, 'Post-Racial' Political Era in America," *NPR*, January 28, 2008.

20. http://www.naacp.org/pages/criminal-justice-fact-sheet.

21. http://www.naacp.org/pages/criminal-justice-fact-sheet.

22. The Drug Policy Alliance, "Race and the Drug War".

23. Jaeah Lee, "Driving While Black Has Actually Gotten More Dangerous in the Last 15 Years," *Mother Jones*, April 15, 2015.

24. Ibid.

25. Jason Williamson, "The Orwellian Police Tactic That Targets Black Americans for Simply Existing," *Salon Magazine*, April 15, 2015.

26. "Black Preschoolers Far More Likely to Be Suspended," *NPR*, March 21, 2014.

27. Brent Staples, "At School, It Matters if You're White or Black," *The New York Times*, March 28, 2014.

28. Mahzarin R. Banaji and Anthony G. Greenwald, *Blindspot: The Hidden Biases of Good People*, Delacorte Press, February 12, 2013.

29. Ryan Gabrielson, Ryann Grochowski Jones, and Eric Sagara, "Deadly Force, in Black and White," *ProPublica*, October 10, 2014.

30. K. D. Kinzler and E. S. Spelke, "Do Infants Show Social Preferences for People Differing in Race?" *Cognition*, 2011, 119(1), pp. 1–9.

31. A. S. Baron and M. R. Banaji, "The Development of Implicit Attitudes: Evidence of Race Evaluations from Ages, 6, 10, and Adulthood," *Psychological Science*, 2006, 17(1), pp. 53–58.

32. Kids' Test Answers on Race Bring Mother to Tears," *CNN*, March 25, 2010.

33. Phillip Jordan and Maria Hernandez-Reif, "Reexamination of Young Children's Racial Attitudes and Skin Tone Preferences," *Journal of Black Psychology*, 2009, 35(3), p. 388.

34. "Study: White and Black Children Biased Toward Lighter Skin," *CNN*, May 14, 2010.

35. Mays, Johnson, Coles, Gellene, Cochran, "Using the Science of Psychology to Target Perpetrators of Racism and Race-Based Discrimination for Intervention Efforts: Preventing Another Trayvon Martin Tragedy," J Soc Action Couns Psychol. 2013 Mar 22; 5(1): 11-36.

36. P. A. Goff, J. L. Eberhardt, M. J., Williams, and M. C. Jackson, "Not Yet Human: Implicit Knowledge, Historical Dehumanization, and Contemporary Consequences," *Journal of Personality and Social Psychology*, 2008, 94, pp. 292–306.

37. Stanford University, "Discrimination Against Blacks Linked to Dehumanization, Study Finds," February 8, 2008, *Science Daily*.

38. Ibid.

39. Ibid.

40. Shawn T. Wahl, "Understanding the African-American Student Experience in Higher Education Through a Relational Dialectics Perspective".

41. Ibid.

42. Karen D. Pyke, "What Is Internalized Racial Oppression and Why Don't We Study It? Acknowledging Racism's Hidden Injuries," *Sociological Perspectives*, 2010, 53(4), pp. 551–557.

43. Ibid.

44. Ibid.

45. Dr. Terry Matthews, "Religious Life in the United States," Lecture Series.

46. Ibid.

47. Nathan Hatch, *The Democratization of American Christianity*, Yale University Press, 1989, p. 222.

48. Anne H. Pinn and Anthony B. Pinn, *Fortress Introduction to Black Church History*, Augsburg Books, 2001, p. 7.

49. Demetrius K. Williams, *An End to This Strife: The Politics of Gender in African American Churches*, Augsberg Fortress, p. 80.

50. Ibid.

51. Stephen R. Haynes, *Noah's Curse*, Oxford University Press, 2002, p. 7

52. Frederick Douglass, *Narrative of the Life of Frederick Douglass, an American Slave*, Appendix.

53. Stephen R. Haynes, *Noah's Curse*, Oxford University Press, 2002, p. 195.

54. Anne H. Pinn and Anthony B. Pinn, *Fortress Introduction to Black Church History*, Augsburg Fortress, 2001, p. 31.

55. Michael Battle, *The Black Church in America: African American Christian Spirituality*, Wiley, 2006, p. 48.

56. Ibid.

57. Andrew F. Walls, *Africa and Christian Identity*, in *Mission Focus* Vol 6 No. 7 (November 1978), p. 12.

58. Kwame Bediako, *Cry Jesus! Christian Theology and Presence in Modern Africa*, The Laing Lecture for 1993.

59. Yaw Acheampong, "Remove Fake 'White' Pictures of Jesus, They Are Responsible for Africa's Dependency on Europeans—Methodist Ministers," *Modern Ghana*, May 7, 2014.

60. Andrew Walls, *The Missionary Movement in Christian History: Studies in the Transmission of Faith*, Orbis Books, 1996, pp. 22–23.

61. Shankar Vedantam, "Psychiatry Ponders Whether Extreme Bias Can Be an Illness," *Washington Post*, December 10, 2005.

62. Philip Cohen, "Who's Afraid of Young Black Men?" *The Atlantic*, July 15, 2013.

63. *Jubilee: The Emergence of African-American Culture*, Schomburg Center for Research in Black Culture.

64. Nikole Hannah-Jones, "Segregation Now . . . ," *The Atlantic*, May 2014.

65. Ibid.

66. Ibid.

67. Jennifer Agiesta and Sonya Ross, "AP Poll: Majority Harbor Prejudice Against Blacks," October 28, 2012.

68. Leonce Gaiter, "After Ferguson: Life Through Black Eyes," *Newsweek*, December 11, 2014.

69. "A Look at Fifth Grade in California Public Schools and the Common Core State Standards," California Department of Education.

70. W.E.B. Du Bois, *Black Reconstruction*, 1835.

71. Christopher Ingraham, "Our Infant Mortality Rate Is a National Embarrassment," *Washington Post*, September 29, 2014.

72. Eric Foner, *The Story of American Freedom*, W.W. Norton, 1999, p. 33.

73. Ibid.

74. Ibid., pp. 33–34.

75. Ta-Nehisi Coates, "The Case for Reparations," *Atlantic Monthly*, June 2014.